The Heritage Corridor

The Heritage Corridor argues for a transnational approach to investigating and recording heritage places that emerge from histories of migration. Addressing the material legacy of migration, this book also relates it to issues of contemporary importance.

Presenting an image of the built environment of migration as one shaped by the ongoing flows of people, ideas, objects and money that circulate through migration corridors, Byrne proposes that houses and other structures built by migrants in their home villages in China over the period 1840–1940 should be seen as crystallisations of the labour, aspirations and longings enacted and experienced by their builders while overseas. Demonstrating that the material world of the migrant is distributed across transnational space, the book calls for an approach to the heritage of migration that is similarly expansive. It proposes and illustrates new methods and strategies for heritage practice.

The Heritage Corridor is a book for scholars and students in the fields of critical heritage studies, migration studies and Chinese diasporic mobilities. It is designed to be accessible to heritage practitioners, readers with an interest in the material worlds of migration, past and present, and to all those with an interest in the 'archaeology' of transnational migration.

Denis Byrne is Associate Professor at the Institute for Culture and Society, Western Sydney University. With a focus on Asia and Australia, he works across the fields of archaeology, critical heritage studies and the environmental humanities, currently with a particular interest in heritage-making by recent migrant and coastal reclamations as an Anthropocene legacy. His most recent book is *Counterheritage: Critical Perspectives on Heritage Conservation in Asia*.

Routledge Research on Museums and Heritage in Asia
Series Editors: Cangbai Wang, Natsuko Akagawa and Denis Byrne

This new and thought-provoking series provides readers with the latest thinking on museums and heritage across Asia and the Asian diaspora. The series will fill a gap in existing museum and heritage scholarship by focusing on voices and perspectives beyond the Western experience. The series is interested in, but not limited to, issues of postcolonialism, decolonisation, mobility, cultural encounters, urbanisation, and digital technology that underpin the rapid transformation of Asia today and shape its future. With contributions from international experts, titles in the series will be relevant to those working across a wide range of disciplines.

The following list includes only the most-recent titles to publish within the series. For more information about the mission of the series and a full list of titles, visit: www.routledge.com/Routledge-Research-on-Museums-and-Heritage-in-Asia/book-series/RRMHA

The Heritage Corridor

A Transnational Approach to the Heritage
of Chinese Migration

Denis Byrne

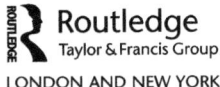

Routledge
Taylor & Francis Group

LONDON AND NEW YORK

First published 2022
by Routledge
2 Park Square, Milton Park, Abingdon, Oxon OX14 4RN

and by Routledge
605 Third Avenue, New York, NY 10158

Routledge is an imprint of the Taylor & Francis Group, an informa business

British Library Cataloguing-in-Publication Data
A catalogue record for this book is available from the British Library

Library of Congress Cataloging-in-Publication Data
A catalog record for this book has been requested

ISBN: 978-0-367-54315-0 (hbk)
ISBN: 978-0-367-54317-4 (pbk)
ISBN: 978-1-003-08871-4 (ebk)

DOI: 10.4324/9781003088714

Typeset in Times New Roman
by Apex CoVantage, LLC

For my sister, Pauline Byrne

Contents

Figures

Acknowledgements

While this book was written entirely by myself and represents my own interpretation of the evidence, it belongs within the context of a larger project (funded by the Australian Research Council under grant DP170101200) which was a multi-disciplinary collaborative effort between myself, Ien Ang (cultural studies and Chinese diaspora studies), Michael Williams (Chinese migration history), Alexandra Wong (urban studies and diaspora studies) and Christopher Cheng (heritage studies), all from the Institute for Culture and Society at Western Sydney University. Their expertise and insights, including in the form of publications cited in the book, have shaped my own perspective on the history and heritage of the Zhongshan–Australia migration corridor. I particularly acknowledge their comradeship during fieldwork in Zhongshan during the period 2017–2019 and, in the case of Alexandra Wong and Christopher Cheng, their fluency in Cantonese and Mandarin, which made the fieldwork possible. Thanks are also due to Ian Johnson for advice on use of the Heurist research database.

I also wish to thank all of those people in Sydney who migrated from Zhongshan County, or are descended from people who did, who agreed to participate in interviews as part of the research that forms the background to this book. In recounting their own or their ancestors' experiences of migration, they gave life and substance to the concept of a Zhongshan–Australia heritage corridor. In drawing on their knowledge of individual migrant pathways that reach back into the emigrant villages of Zhongshan (a former county, now a prefecture, in southeast Guangdong), they helped make it possible to locate and document ancestral houses, lineage halls and other buildings there which they have direct or indirect links to. In Zhongshan itself, thanks are due to the numerous people who generously provided information and guidance, particularly in regard to the built heritage of those who migrated to Australia between the 1840s and 1940s. These include King Chow of the Zhongshan branch of the Bureau of Chinese Overseas Affairs, Chen Di Qui (historian and former employee of the Bureau, Gan Jian Bo (heritage architect), and Anthony Liang (historian), all of whom were as generous with their specialist knowledge as they were with their hospitality.

I also thank the Institute for Culture and Society, Western Sydney University for providing administrative support for the project, and my academic colleagues at the Institute who have helped make it a wonderful place to be based. Phillip Mar provided invaluable editorial comments on late drafts of the book. Last but not least, my boundless gratitude is due to Daniel Ng for his personal support, humour and understanding over the years.

Introduction

Every night the lights are switched on in vacant houses in a village in the Batangas region of the Philippines in order to lend the houses and the village a 'happy atmosphere' (Aguilar 2009: 104). The houses were built by the large proportion of the village's population living and working overseas, mainly in Italy and Spain. Filomena Aguilar tells us that some of the villagers who participated in his ethnographic research say the lighting up of the houses at night, paid for by the overseas owners, 'prevents ghosts from colonizing the house' and may also be

> a way of communicating to the house itself, assuring it that it has not been abandoned and should not feel miserable – as if the house were an animate entity, consistent with the way houses are commonly understood in the Southeast Asian worldview.
>
> (Aguilar 2009: 104)

Despite the geographic distance separating them, the houses and their overseas owners are seen to extend into each other across transnational space, leading lives at either end of a Philippines–Mediterranean migration corridor that reveals itself to be a social-material continuum.

Migration heritage in transnational perspective

Transnational connectivity of this kind is common to the numerous migration corridors that criss-cross the globe today, just as they did a century ago, although there were fewer of them then and the circulatory traffic of people, ideas, commodities and money passing along them was a good deal slower. This book's concern is with the migration corridor as a transnational field of material heritage, a field populated by the physical traces of the migration experience primarily in the form of not only buildings and portable

DOI: 10.4324/9781003088714-1

artefacts but also including streets and market gardens. Among the buildings are houses and business premises that were occupied by migrants in their destination country as well as the houses they built for themselves and their relatives back in their 'home' villages or towns, using money earned overseas and remitted back – hence the term 'remittance houses'. It has often been the case that through the phenomenon of serial migration, a large portion of the population of a village in a migrant-sending country such as China, Lebanon or Mexico ends up residing in a particular suburb, town or region in a receiving country, giving rise to Appadurai's (1996) concept of a transnational 'ethnoscape'. From the 1990s, migration scholars have studied the connectivity and co-dependency of individuals and families across migration corridors and the implications of this for their identity, gender relations and political participation (Glick Schiller and Caglar 2013; Ong 1999; Vertovec 2004).

The transnationalist turn in migration studies occurred in the 1990s as a rebuttal of what Levitt and Glick Schiller (2004: 1005) have called the 'unilinear assimilationist paradigm,' which between the 1920s and 1980s and particularly in the USA had concentrated attention on the ways migrants progressively adapted to conditions in their destination places and assimilated into the majority culture there, often in the face of regulations and social forces that sought to exclude them (Vertovec 2001: 574). Here, migration was implicitly conceived as a one-way journey. The new attention to the transnational dimension of migration not only revealed the extent to which migrants typically maintain cross-border relations with people and places in their origin place but also showed that this is not incompatible with the development ties of belonging in their destination locale. In her influential essay 'Home and Away', Sara Ahmed (1999: 342), in describing home as embodied consciousness rather than an entity that exists in its own right, went so far as to say, 'it is impossible to return to a place that was lived as home, precisely because the home is not exterior to a self, but implicated in it.' Return is indeed impossible, in the sense that we are never able to return to a previous state of being, never able to reinhabit a place the way we used to, but millions of migrants have made regular visits back to their places of origin, have built or renovated houses there, dreamt of retiring there and have participated remotely in the social, economic and political life of the villages, towns and countries they came from. This has immense implications for a practice of heritage that takes migration as its subject.

The concepts of dual belonging and of origin and destination places having simultaneous presence in migrant lives are now well established in scholarly thinking on migration (Levitt and Glick Schiller 2004; Tsuda 2012). And yet the idea of transnational simultaneity has not been taken up to any significant extent in heritage practice. One reason, I suggest, is that the conventional notion of the heritage place as fixed, stable and situated in the kind of Cartesian geometric space which Lefebvre (1991: 14) calls 'isotropic', acts to obstruct it. This has much to do with the emergence of the heritage idea in the discursive context of 19th-century nation-building in which material heritage was conceived as the patrimony of a particular territorialised group, the 'imagined community' of the nation (Anderson 1991). The historically embedded notion of the nation-state as the container of society (Taylor 1994), which I argue is formative to the conception of heritage as a field of practice, is incompatible with what we know of the way transnational migrants live their lives (e.g., Levitt and Glick Schiller 2004). It is alien to what Lozanovska (2019: 205) refers to as the transborder 'psychic landscape' within which migrants dwell. In Ien Ang's words (2011: 87), 'Diaspora poses a problem for . . . authorised national heritage because it is by definition a denationalising, transnationalising force.' The 'problem' that heritage has in grasping the transnational dimension of the material past of migration is illustrated by the fact that the two recent books that *do* grasp it, namely Sarah Lopez's (2015) *The Remittance Landscape* and Mirjana Lozanovska's (2019) *Migrant Housing: Architecture, Dwelling, Migration*, come not from the field of heritage but from that of architecture. In recent work, I have attempted to chart a path into the materiality of migration, in all its cross-border fluidity, from a heritage studies perspective (Byrne 2016a, 2016b, 2020).

Before proceeding further, it is important to be clear about what is meant by the term 'heritage' as it is used in this book. The book is concerned with objects and places associated with migration in the past. These, to the extent that they survive into the present, constitute the material traces of migration. While it would be accurate to refer to them simply as 'old things' or as the 'material past', I refer to them as 'heritage' partly in recognition that in popular usage the term has become a kind of shorthand for the material record of the past but also because I am concerned with what this material record means to people in the present. It is neither possible nor desirable, however, to dodge the reality that the term 'heritage' implies valuation. Old places and things become heritage via processes of valuation that are enmeshed in the social, political and economic environment of the present. The field of critical heritage studies was founded on the argument that old things are not valuable in their own right and most critical scholarship on heritage over the last 50 years or so has focused on the power dynamics of heritage valuation – on how, for example, the Global North has through discursive and technocratic means been able to assert its own regime of value over the material past of the Global South. The work of heritage bureaucrats and experts, while ostensibly concerned simply with protecting and conserving heritage, implicitly serves to privilege certain old things over certain others – it is never value-neutral.

Caitlin DeSilvey and Rodney Harrison (2020: 3) observe that

> scholarship in critical heritage and museum studies has been important in showing how heritage "works" to promote certain kinds of objects, places, practices and values to the detriment of others – heritage generates its own particular systems of value which emerge from specific collecting and ordering practices.

The system of value that a 'bordered' approach to migration heritage adopts is one that privileges narratives of arrival, adaptation, settlement and unitary belonging over those of ongoing transnational mobility and multiple belonging. The objects this system produces include, for example, sites of migrant arrival such as Ellis Island in New York and the Quarantine Station on Sydney Harbour, both celebrated as nationally significant heritage places. Sites of return that it ignores include, for example, the villages in Mexico in which over the last century millions of Mexican migrants in the USA have built houses, churches and schools (Lopez 2015). These are villages many migrants revisit regularly and maintain close relations of belonging with. Such places seem absent from the national imaginary of migrant-receiving countries. They are absent from the heritage inventories of these countries as sites which, despite lying beyond their territorial borders, are of vital connective significance to a large proportion of their citizens. I attribute such excisions in large part to the effects of a 'methodological nationalism' (Gielis 2009; Levitt and Glick Schiller 2004) wherein heritage practice defaults to the nation-state as the unit of analysis.

The proposition behind this book is that the heritage landscape of transnational migration is necessarily transnational – it is the material dimension of the cross-border social field inhabited by the migrant. The term 'transnational heritage' is employed here because of its mainstream legibility; Christian Rossipal (2021), however, makes a good case for the alternative term 'transversal heritage', arguing that the heritage at issue here emerges from a cross-border fluidity that, following Soguk and Whitehall (1999), represents a condition that is a 'prior, anterior ground' to that of the nation. He sees transversal heritage as a 'counterheritage' (Byrne 2014) project, one which is not against the idea of heritage as such but 'against heritage as it is generally construed within the paradigm of the nation-state' (Rossipal 2021: 45–46).

Over the past two decades, there has been significant interest in the subject of modern-era migration among heritage scholars, historians and museologists (Anheier and Isar 2011; Colomer and Catalani 2020; Darien-Smith and Hamilton 2019; Dellios and Henrich 2020; Holtorf, Pantazatos and Scarre 2018; Wang 2021). This work affords recognition to the fact that for a significant proportion of the world's population, their cultural heritage emerges in a state of mobility and transience, but it is not aimed at bringing into view the transnationally stretched landscape of migration heritage. Other work, in the field of the archaeology of the contemporary past, addresses itself to the 'illegal' passage across nation-state borders by migrants (De León 2012; Soto 2018), to migrant border camps (Hicks and Mallet 2019; Kourelis 2019) and to the material world of undocumented migrants more generally (Hamilakis 2018), often bringing a careful and forensic attention to bear on physical traces of the experiences of endurance, suffering and death which occur in such border spaces.

The Heritage Corridor joins this broad effort to bring the subject of migration, with all its connotations of mobility, dislocation and placemaking, into the field of heritage practice. However, the book's particular attention is on the migration corridor as a site of heritage. As noted earlier, heritage practice has tended to privilege the geographic fixity of objects. In the chapters that follow, the place of the migrant is, by contrast, shown to be constituted in cross-border circulatory flows of people, ideas, goods and money. It is a place that is not merely situated in transnational space, it is constitutive of it (Byrne 2016a, 2016b).

The Zhongshan–Australia heritage corridor

There is a contradiction apparent in the efforts of sovereign states to promote a sense of cohesive, unitary identity across their population while at the same time enforcing border policies that treat sometimes large segments of the population within their borders as outsiders. From the late 1800s in the West's settler colonies – Canada, the USA, Australia, New Zealand and South Africa – anti-Asian immigration restrictions began to be imposed (McKeown 2011). In place until the period between the 1950s and 1970s, these discriminatory policies are particularly relevant for the present study because they reinforced transnational ties and a sense of dual identity among Chinese migrants. In Australia, for example, immigration restrictions imposed from the 1890s and collectively known as the White Australia policy meant that the wives and children of Chinese men were unable to enter the country, a situation that often meant frequent return visits by these men to their home villages, high rates of remittance sending, the channelling of income into the building of new houses and modern infrastructure in the home villages and, in some cases, the transferring back to

China of businesses founded in Australia (Fitzgerald 2007; Williams 2018). Immigration restrictions thus enhanced the cross-border simultaneity of Chinese migrant lives which translates into a high degree of interconnectivity between migrant-associated heritage places at either end of the migration corridor. In today's world, the increased numbers of undocumented migrants and migrants on temporary visas has a similar effect of fostering transnational lifeways. Both as a historical and contemporary phenomenon, this calls for a practice of heritage able to break with the habit of methodological nationalism.

The heritage corridor concept is useful in showing that the material record of migration is not just distributed transnationally but also *oriented* that way. In Sara Ahmed's (2006: 9) phenomenology, spaces and objects are not exterior to bodies; they fold into each other and are oriented towards each other. Ahmed's (2006: 29–30) account of the way that people and things are 'impressed' on each other assists an understanding of early 20th-century remittance houses in Guangdong as being oriented towards those Chinese migrants in Honolulu, Sydney and elsewhere who thought of them, dreamt of them and laboured to earn money to construct them. The houses and their builders, however remote they were geographically, were mutually enfolded, fitting into each other in a way that does justice to the 'diasporic state of mind' (Ang 2011: 86) wherein via long-distance memories, attachments and senses of belonging, migrants commonly experience home and away simultaneously.[1]

The particular focus of this book is the migration corridor stretching between Zhongshan (Heung San in Cantonese), a county situated in Guangdong's Pearl River Delta, and Australia (Figure 0.1). By 1860, there were 25,000 people in Victoria from villages in the Pearl River Delta and a further 13,000 in New South Wales, most of them on the goldfields (Williams 2018: 49). Zhongshan migrants in Australia, overwhelmingly male, later came to be concentrated in New South Wales and Queensland, nearly 1,500 being resident in New South Wales by the 1920s (Williams 2018: 37). After the Gold Rush petered out in the 1860s and 1870s, Zhongshan migrants became market gardeners, storekeepers, importers, restaurateurs, furniture-makers and wholesalers of bananas and other produce. In Chapter 1, I describe the material world of these people from the perspective of their individual lives and the particular material continuities that those lives gave rise to across the Zhongshan–Australia migration corridor. The active involvement of many Zhongshan migrants in Australia in construction projects in their home villages and, at a broader level, their continued engagement with and attachment to the built environment of their home county, prompts the idea that migrant-associated buildings at both ends of the migration corridor are distributed entities, a material counterpart of the transnationally

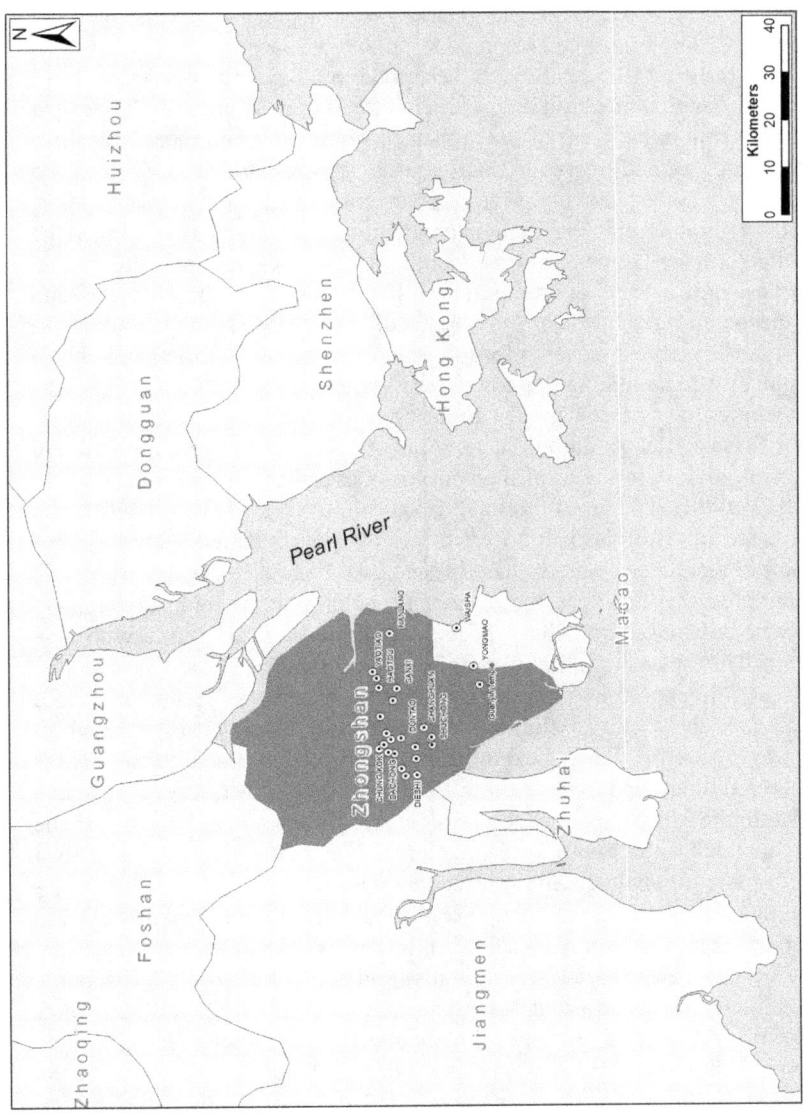

Figure 0.1 Map of Zhongshan showing some of the villages which sent migrants to Australia.

distributed personhood of migrants. This idea is further developed in Chapter 2. Although their foundations are sunk in the soil of particular countries, these buildings are elements of social-material assemblages stretched across transnational space. The chapter also considers ways in which the affectivity of buildings can resonate through this space.

From the mid-19th century, as described in Chapter 3, by far the most obvious change to the built environment of emigrant villages in Zhongshan County came in the form of the numerous houses that migrants built there with money earned overseas. Such houses, typically much larger than the houses of villagers lacking migrant connections and, from the late 1800s, increasingly different from them in architectural style, radically changed the architectural landscape of migrant-sending areas of Guangdong and Fujian. They are now a focus of attention both for Chinese heritage managers and for diaspora tourists. Much of the fieldwork conducted in the emigrant villages as background research for this book consisted of locating and photographically documenting these houses (Figure 0.2).

Attention turns in Chapter 4 to an often-neglected aspect of the heritage of transnational migration, religion, specifically the religion Chinese migrants took with them on their journeys overseas. An account is given of the way that Chinese migrants, to varying degrees, have related to the landscape of their destination countries by merging their own religious beliefs and practices with the existing sacred topography they have entered. Essential to this has been the manner in which popular and miraculously efficacious Chinese gods have become established in and fused with new terrain. The particular mobility of this form of popular religion has assisted Chinese migrants to live in overseas settings by creating secondary sacred landscapes there, not dissimilar to the way the relocation of relics from the Christian Holy Land, beginning in the 6th century, enabled a secondary sacred landscape to develop in Europe (Geary 1986). Attention is also drawn to the role of the lineage in Chinese migration and particularly to the way in which the decay of ancestral halls in home villages acts as a catalyst for diaspora involvement in projects of restoration.

In the countries of the Global North to which Chinese have migrated in large numbers since the mid-1900s, religion has been an aspect of the Chinese culture seized upon in Orientalist and social evolutionist discourse to characterise the migrants as representatives of an archaic and timeless world. Chapter 5 examines the phenomenon in which these migrants, although themselves identifying as modern subjects, participated in the creation of Chinatowns in Canada, the USA and Australia. In Australia, these Orientalist constructions have become metaphors for multicultural inclusiveness, but a more critical reading of them suggests they function to prop up the idea held by many in the white majority that an immutable

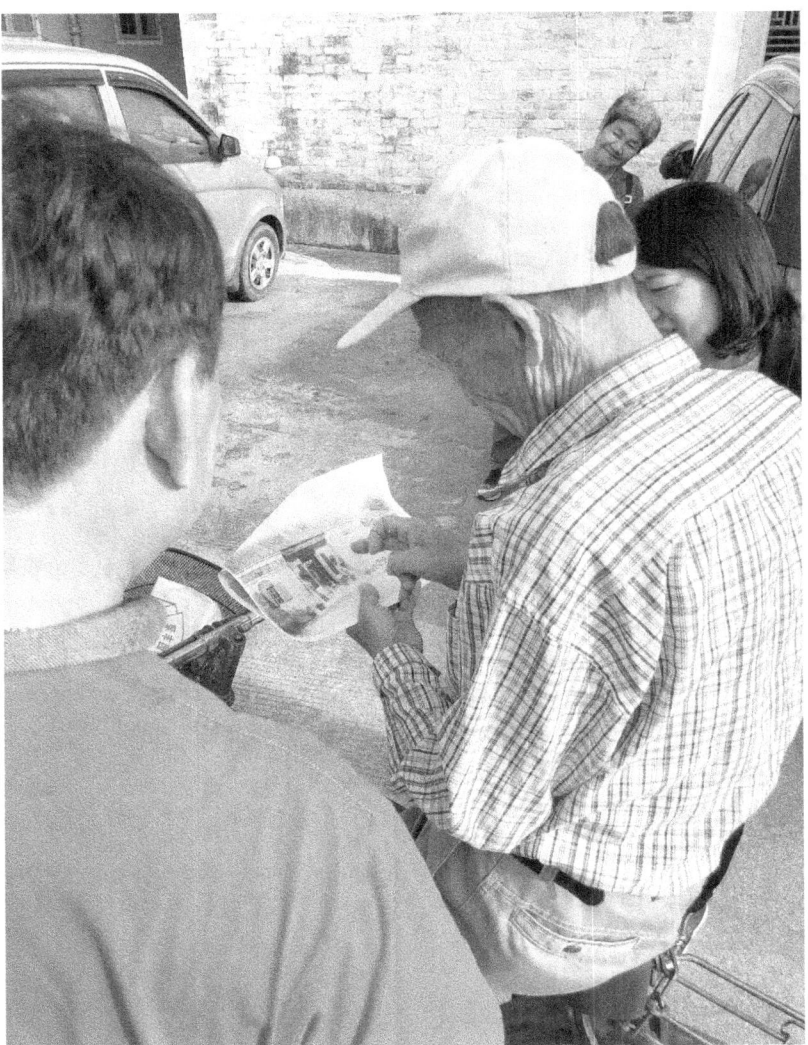

Figure 0.2 An elderly resident of Wushi village, Zhongshan, examines a photograph of the ancestral house of Henry Fine (Ah Hing) who left Wushi for Australia in 1877. The house appears not to have survived into the present day.

'core' Anglo culture persists in the midst of the kind of non-white immigrant 'difference' that multiculturalism celebrates. It is proposed that core culture has its equivalent in the phenomenon of *core heritage*, the product of an institutionalised heritage practice that implicitly privileges the 'original' Anglo-Australian architectural identity of buildings over the ways that non-Anglo migrants have adapted them to their purposes and lifestyles.

The book concludes with an argument for the advantages a 'heritage corridor' approach to the material record of migration has over the nation-bound frame that has been conventional in heritage practice. Tim Ingold's (2011, 2017) meshwork concept is drawn upon to help move towards a heritage practice that can better represent the fluidity and mobility of past migrant lives. In Ingold's conception, human lives flow along lines that intersect at points he describes as 'knots', the lines and knots forming a meshwork. Describing the meshwork as 'an unbounded entanglement of lines in fluid space' (Ingold 2011: 64), he is at pains to show that the knots of the meshwork are not places where lines begin and end but rather are points at which they converge, passing under and over each other before moving on. If we think of the knots in the trajectories of migrant lives as taking the form of buildings or unbuilt sites such as market gardens, Ingold's meshwork model implicitly cautions against them being allowed to take precedence, in heritage representation, over the lines that connect them. In other words, we should be striving for an approach to the heritage of migrancy that is fluid and mobile enough to be able to follow migrant lives across the boundaries of sites, nations and racial categorisations, transcending the limits that conventional thinking in the heritage field imposes on how those lives are represented. That is this book's ambition.

Note

1   In addition to the 'remittance houses' built at the direction of migrants located off-shore, some were constructed by migrants who had returned to live in Zhongshan (or Hong Kong) or were built during visits 'home'.

References

Aguilar, Filomeno. 2009. 'Labour migration and ties of relatedness: Diasporic houses and investments in memory in a rural Philippine village,' *Thesis Eleven* 98: 88–114, https://doi.org/10.1177/0725513609105485.

Ahmed, Sara. 1999. 'Home and away: Narratives of migration and estrangement,' *International Journal of Cultural Studies* 2(3): 329–347, https://doi.org/10.1177/136787799900200303.

Ahmed, Sara. 2006. *Queer Phenomenology: Orientations, Objects, Others*. Durham, NC: Duke University Press.

Anderson, Benedict. 1991. *Imagined Communities: Reflections on the Origin and Spread of Nationalism*. Ithaca, NY: Cornell University Press

Ang, Ien. 2011. 'Unsettling the national: Heritage and diaspora,' in Helmut Anheier and Yudhishthir Raj Isar (eds.), *Heritage, Memory and Identity*, pp. 82–94. London: Sage.

Anheier, Helmut and Yudhishthir Raj Isar (eds.). 2011. *Heritage, Memory and Identity*. London: Sage.

Appadurai, Arjun. 1996. *Modernity at Large: Cultural Dimensions of Globalization*. Minneapolis: University of Minnesota Press.

Byrne, Denis. 2014. *Counterheritage: Critical Perspectives on Heritage Conservation in Asia*. New York: Routledge.

Byrne, Denis. 2016a. 'Heritage corridors: Transnational flows and the built environment of migration,' *Journal of Ethnic and Migration Studies* 42(14): 2351–2369, https://doi.org/10.1080/1369183X.2016.1205805.

Byrne, Denis. 2016b. 'The need for a transnational approach to the material heritage of migration: The China-Australia corridor,' *Journal of Social Archaeology* 16(3): 61–85, https://doi.org/10.1177/1469605316673005.

Byrne, Denis. 2020. 'Dream houses in China: Migrant-built houses in Zhongshan County (1890s–1940) as a "distributed" form of heritage,' *Fabrications* 30(2): 176–201, https://doi.org/10.1080/10331867.2020.1749218.

Colomer, Laia and Anna Catalani (eds.). 2020. *Heritage Discourses in Europe: Responding to Migration, Mobility, and Cultural Identities in the Twenty-First Century*. Amsterdam: Arc Humanities Press.

Darien-Smith, Kate and Paula Hamilton. 2019. *Remembering Migration: Oral History and Heritage in Australia*. London: Palgrave Macmillan.

De León, Jason. 2012. ' "Better to be hot than caught": Excavating the conflicting roles of migrant material culture,' *American Anthropologist* 114(3): 477–495, https://doi.org/10.1111/j.1548-1433.2012.01447.x.

Dellios, Alexandra and Eureka Henrich (eds.). 2020. *Migrant, Multicultural and Diasporic Heritage: Beyond and Between Borders*. London: Routledge.

DeSilvey, Caitlin and Rodney Harrison. 2020. 'Anticipating loss: Rethinking endangerment in heritage futures,' *International Journal of Heritage Studies* 26(1): 1–7, https://doi.org/10.1080/13527258.2019.1644530.

Fitzgerald, John. 2007. *Big White Lie: Chinese Australians in White Australia*. Sydney: University of New South Wales Press.

Geary, Patrick J. 1986. 'Sacred commodities: The circulation of medieval relics,' in Arjun Appadurai (ed.), *The Social Life of Things: Commodities in Cultural Perspective*, pp. 169–192. Cambridge: Cambridge University Press.

Gielis, Ruben. 2009. 'A global sense of migrant places: Towards a place perspective in the study of migrant transnationalism,' *Global Networks* 9(2): 271–287, https://doi.org/10.1111/j.1471-0374.2009.00254.x

Glick Schiller, Nina and Ayse Caglar. 2013. 'Locating migrant pathways of economic emplacement: Thinking beyond the ethnic lens,' *Ethnicities* 13(4): 494–514, https://doi.org/10.1177/1468796813483733.

Hamilakis, Yannis (ed.). 2018. *The New Nomadic Age: Archaeologies of Forced and Undocumented Migration*. Sheffield: Equinox.

Hicks, Dan and Sarah Mallet. 2019. *Lande: The Calais 'Jungle' and Beyond*. Bristol: Bristol University Press.

Holtorf, Cornelius, Andreas Pantazatos and Geoffrey Scarre (eds.). 2018. *Cultural Heritage and Contemporary Migrations*. London: Routledge.

Ingold, Tim. 2011. *Being Alive: Essays on Movement, Knowledge and Description*. Abingdon, UK: Routledge.

Ingold, Tim. 2017. 'On human correspondence,' *Journal of the Royal Anthropological Institute* 23(1): 9–27, https://doi.org/10.1111/1467-9655.12541.

Kourelis, Kostis 2019. 'Sites of refuge in a historically layered landscape: Camps in central Greece,' *Change Over Time* 9(1): 88–113, https://doi.org/10.1353/cot.2019.0006.

Lefebvre, Henri. 1991. *The Production of Space*, translated by Donald Nicholson-Smith. Oxford: Blackwell.

Levitt, Peggy and Nina Glick Schiller. 2004. 'Conceptualizing simultaneity: A transnational social field perspective on society,' *International Migration Review* 38(3): 1002–1039, https://doi.org /10.1111/j.1747-7379.2004.tb00227.x.

Lopez, Sarah. 2015. *The Remittance Landscape: Spaces of Migration in Rural Mexico and Urban USA*. Chicago: University of Chicago Press.

Lozanovska, Mirjana. 2019. *Migrant Housing: Architecture, Dwelling, Migration*. London: Routledge.

McKeown, Adam M. 2011. *Melancholy Order: Asian Migration and the Globalization of Borders*. New York: Columbia University Press.

Ong, Aihwa. 1999. *Flexible Citizenship: The Cultural Logic of Transnationalism*. Durham, NC: Duke University Press.

Rossipal, Christian. 2021. 'The noncitizen archive: Transversal heritage and the jurisgenerative process,' in Alexandra Dellios and Eureka Henrich (eds.), *Migrant, Multicultural and Diasporic Heritage: Beyond and Between Borders*, pp. 36–51. London: Routledge, https://doi.org 10.4324/9780429328404.

Soguk, Nevzat and Geoffrey Whitehall. 1999. 'Wandering grounds: Transversality, identity, territoriality, and movement,' *Millennium: Journal of International Studies* 28(3): 675–698, https://doi.org/10.1177/03058298990280030301.

Soto, Gabriella. 2018. 'Object afterlives and the burden of history: Between "trash" and "heritage" in the steps of migrants,' *American Anthropologist* 120(3): 460–473, https://doi.org/10.1111/aman.13055

Taylor, Peter J. 1994. 'The state as container: Territoriality in the modern world-system,' *Progress in Human Geography* 18(2): 151–162, https://doi.org/10.1177/030913259401800202.

Tsuda, Takeyuki. 2012. 'Whatever happened to simultaneity? Transnational migration theory and dual engagement in send and receiving countries,' *Journal of Ethnic and Migration Studies* 38(4): 631–649, https://doi.org/10.1080/1369183X.2012.659126.

Vertovec, Stephen. 2001. 'Transnationalism and identity,' *Journal of Ethnic and Migration Studies* 27(4): 573–582, https://doi.org/10.1080/13691830120090386.

Vertovec, Stephen. 2004. 'Migrant transnationalism and modes of transformation,' *International Migration Review* 38(4): 970–1001, https://doi.org/10.1111/j.1747-7379.2004.tb00226.x

Wang, Cangbai. 2021. *Museum Representations of Chinese Diasporas: Migration Histories and the Cultural Heritage of the Homeland.* London: Routledge.

Williams, Michael. 2018. *Returning Home with Glory: Chinese Villagers Around the Pacific, 1849 to 1949.* Hong Kong: Hong Kong University Press.

1 Transborder lives and materialities

The approach to migrant heritage advocated in this book is one in which migrant lives and migrant materialities are considered to be mutually constituted and as forming a social-material continuum. It follows that any study of migrant heritage should draw upon whatever historical sources are available, including oral and documentary histories, in addition to surveying and interrogating the material record.

Historians and anthropologists have confirmed the transnational character of migrant subjectivity. The relevance of their research to the development of a transnational approach to migrant heritage lies in the attention many of them devote to the spatiality and materiality of migration. In writing of the history of the China–Canada migration corridor, Henry Yu (2011: 404) draws attention to the 'vast rhythm of transpacific movement' that since the early 19th century has constituted what he refers to as the Cantonese Pacific: 'a network of circular movements [that] tied small villages to port cities and urban enclaves on both sides of the ocean.' For him and other historians of Chinese migration, 'the site' of migration is seen to be transnational in scope. In Madeline Hsu's (2000) history of the migration to the USA from Taishan County in south-eastern Guangdong between 1882 and 1943, for example, she devotes detailed attention to the things – houses, roads, railroads, schools and factories – that the returned migrants built in Taishan and that Taishanese in the USA contributed funds for.

Turning to the China–Australia migration corridor, Kate Bagnall's (2013) study of the links between a village in Xinhui County, Guangdong, and the goldfields settlement of Indigo in north-eastern Victoria is acutely attuned to the geography and the migrant-associated built environment of these places.[1] Bagnall draws extensively on archival sources in Australia in order to trace the migrant trajectories of Chinese–Australians back to their origin villages in the Pearl River Delta, in southern China, often succeeding in relocating their ancestral houses there and conducting oral history interviews with current village residents.[2] The historian Barry McGowan

DOI: 10.4324/9781003088714-2

(2005) has conducted archival research on Chinese migrants in New South Wales, Australia, who operated market gardens between the mid-1800s and mid-1900s, combining this with field research in which he identifies the location of some of the gardens on the basis of surviving crop marks and remains of wooden water races used for irrigating the crops. Such work provides an important resource for any study of the material heritage of the China–Australia migration corridor.

Migrant trajectories and their material traces

From the perspective of Paolo Boccagni (2014: 277–278), 'migrant belong-ing' is an 'open-ended and faceted process,' that informs the 'territorial, social and emotional spaces' of individual migrant biographies. In this chapter, I turn to the biographies of three men who departed Zhongshan County for Australia, two of them in the 1890s, the other in the 1930s (those migrating in this period were overwhelmingly male). The first thing to say about the biographies is that they are constructions that coalesce around fragmentary records, consisting of a limited array of documents and recorded memories. As such they are artefacts of the research process. In the second place, the temporality of the biographies extends across the span of the migrants' own lives and those of their first- and second-generation descendants. One of these migrants, Stanley Hunt (1927–2019) published, with the assistance of his sister, an autobiography (Hunt 2009) late in life. This book, along with an interview with him conducted by myself and my co-researchers in 2017, forms the basis of the biographical sketch presented here. By contrast, almost everything we know of Tim Jang (1881–1952), who migrated from Zhongshan to Queensland in 1998 at the age of 17, comes from the recollections of his descendants and from Australian immi-gration records. Without the determination of his granddaughter in Zhong-shan to piece together what had happened to him in the last decades of his life in Australia, Tim Jang's life as a migrant would have no visibility in the present.[3]

The heritage record of migrant lives is similarly fragmentary. It is reli-ant on the capacity of objects (including buildings) to survive into the pre-sent in recognisable form and on these objects having attributes that testify to their association with specific migrant lives. In some cases, it is a non-material or documentary trace, such as a memorised or written record of a street address in an emigrant village, that allows an object such as a house to be linked back to a particular migrant. The temporal–spatial trajectories of transnational migrants have taken them not just across national borders but often also through multiple temporary homes and workplaces in their destination countries as they strive to carve out futures for themselves. This plurilocal (Boccagni 2014: 280) existence can be conceptualised in terms of the lines and knots of Ingold's (2007, 2011) theory of meshwork (discussed in Chapter 6). A migrant's trajectories (lines) through the terrain of the destination country intersect with the trajectories, or lifelines, of numerous others. The knots in the meshwork, representing houses and workplaces, for example, are likely to have strands that link back to the origin country, strands representing the flow of letters or remittance transfers, or indeed representing return visits made by the migrants themselves. While the experience of migration has been described as one of home-making in a new country (Boccagni 2014; Boccagni and Erdal 2020), with all the physical and emotional 'work' that home-making entails, this process of localisation typically occurs amid strong ongoing ties to the 'home' of the home country.

The biographies that follow are not to be regarded as discreet trajectories. They are better thought of representing sections of the meshwork of migrancy. But how are we to represent the complex intertwining of mobile lives and plurilocal placemaking in heritage practice? I do not pretend to have a definitive answer to this but aim to provide an idea of what the biographical trajectories of Zhongshan migrants looked like both in narrative form and as arrays of material sites and objects.

Chee Win Lee and his descendants

When Chee Win Lee (1880–1951) arrived in Sydney from Zhongshan County in the late 1900s, he sets about establishing a grocery shop at 82 Harbour Street in the city's Chinatown. Named Yet Shing & Co, the shop was in a single-storey building in a row of similar Chinese-owned shops located just opposite Sydney's main fruit and vegetable market. The market was a sprawling brick building, a landmark in the lives of the 3,680 Chinese recorded in the 1901 census as living in Sydney. Many of Chee Win's customers were Chinese men who, as fruit and vegetable wholesalers and retailers, had stalls in the markets. Others were Chinese market gardeners who brought their produce in to sell at the markets from gardens occupying available plots of undeveloped land in the suburbs. With so many of his customers hailing from his own county and speaking the same Zhongshan dialect of Cantonese, it might at times have seemed to him that he was living in a geographical outlier of Zhongshan. In terms of Ingold's meshwork theory, Chee Win's grocery shop was a small knot in the interwoven lifelines of many immigrants, one that was threaded to the larger knot represented by the markets (Ingold 2011: 83–85). The market building was demolished in the 1970s to make way for a large concrete concert hall that was demolished in 2016 to make way for a complex of high-rise apartments, a large proportion of whose occupants are Chinese–Australians. It is tantalising to think that some of their ancestors worked in or were regular visitors to the markets in the space below their feet.

Like many other men from South China, Chee Win did not apparently regard his decision to depart Zhongshan for Australia as constituting a decision to leave China permanently. Some of his Chinese contemporaries in Australia married white Australian women or women of other ethnicities, including indigenous Aboriginal women, but many opted to return to China to find partners. Chee Win himself sailed back to Zhongshan on a visit when he was 30 and there in 1910 he married Wong See who remained in Shekki when he returned to Sydney. By 1910, anti-Chinese immigration restrictions in Australia would have made it very difficult for him to bring his wife with him. In 1911, Chee Win and Wong See's son, Wah Hook Lee, was born in Shekki and later went to school there. An unintentional result of the Australian immigration laws was that they reinforced the transnational ties that bound Chinese–Australians to their homeland.[4]

Having become a successful store-owner in Australia, it is unsurprising that Chee Win would decide to extend that success back to Zhongshan. Either on his first return there or on a subsequent visit, he bought a shop in a building at 86 Yuelai Road, one of Shekki's main streets (Figure 1.1),

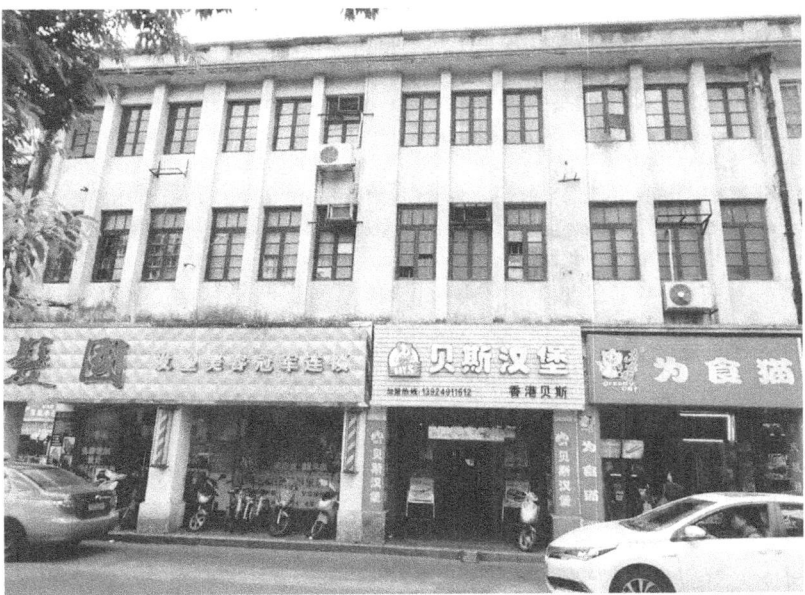

Figure 1.1 Chee Win Lee's former shop in Shekki, Zhongshan (the shop is immediately behind the white car).

establishing a mixed business there. He and his wife built a house nearby at 46 Mei Ji Street. Both the shop and house are still standing, the former technically still owned by his descendants in Sydney. The three-storey brick building that houses the shop, one of Shekki's first modern commercial buildings, has an arcaded ground floor for pedestrian traffic. The arcade is in the style seen in the rows of shophouses that by the beginning of the 19th century were a trademark of Chinese settlement in Singapore, Malacca and other Southeast Asian towns (Yeoh 1996). That the style made its way back to the Pearl River Delta hometowns of many members of the Southeast Asian Chinese diaspora testifies to the enduring social and economic links which migration established between the two regions. The building in Yuelai Road was renovated a few decades ago and although the entire exterior was covered with a new layer of stucco cement, the clean lines of the modernistic façade are still legible.

When the Japanese invaded Guangdong in 1938, Chee Win returned to Zhongshan and succeeded in bringing his wife, his young daughter and his son, Wah Hook, then 18, back to Australia. Wah Hook helped in the family's grocery shop in Sydney until, around 1930, he was sent to school in Honolulu where he stayed with relatives. Hawaii was a key node in the diasporic network of people originating in Zhongshan. After Wah Hook returned to live in Sydney in 1937 he married Doris Gay (1915–2013), the daughter of a Chinese–Australian family also originating in Zhongshan. Soon after their marriage they sailed to Hong Kong and went to live in Shekki for a year, staying at Wah Hook's father's house. Since most Zhongshanese leaving for and returning home from Australia transited through Hong Kong, the city loomed large in the lives of Zhongshan folk in cities like Sydney. It was linked to Shekki via steam ferries and large junks; the sampans that plied the county's many streams carried people and goods onward to the county's many emigrant villages, connecting them to the outside world (Bagnall 2012: 128).

The Japanese invasion of Guangdong in October 1938 and then of Hong Kong in December 1941 effectively terminated travel along the Zhongshan–Australia migration corridor until the Pacific War ended in August 1945. Travel resumed after the war but slowed to a trickle after the founding of the People's Republic of China (PRC) in 1949, not regaining momentum until the advent of Deng Xiaoping's Open Door policy of 1978. This meant that after more than a century in which it was common for the Australian-born children of Chinese parents to travel to Zhongshan and Hong Kong to visit relatives and improve their Cantonese language skills, a generation or two of Chinese–Australians grew up lacking first-hand knowledge of China. And when traffic along the migration corridor resumed after 1978, for many migrant descendants in Australia it took the form of visits of discovery to ancestral locations such as home villages, graveyards, ancestral houses and clan halls, places known to them only through stories told by parents and grandparents.

This was the case for William Lee (1934–), son of Doris and Wah Hook, who visited Zhongshan with his wife Nancy (of British descent) for the first time in the late 1980s (Figure 1.2). They found their way to Xin Cun village, close to Shekki, the birthplace of Williams's grandfather, Chee Win, only to find that the ancestral house was gone, bombed by the Japanese during the war. The house plot now lay under a highway. And during the Mao era, the family's house in Shekki had been divided up, Chee Win's descendants now having title only to one portion of it.

When Nancy Lee retired from her teaching career, she began systematically researching the Lee family's history, assembling birth and marriage certificates, letters, family photographs and other items that formed a documentary counterpart to the family's built heritage, which included the shops in Sydney and Shekki along with a series of houses that have been home to family members in Sydney. A branch of Nancy's research was devoted to the family of the Zhongshan migrant, George Louis Gay, which became linked to the Lee's when his daughter, Doris, married Wah Hook, Chee Win Lee's son, in Sydney in 1937.

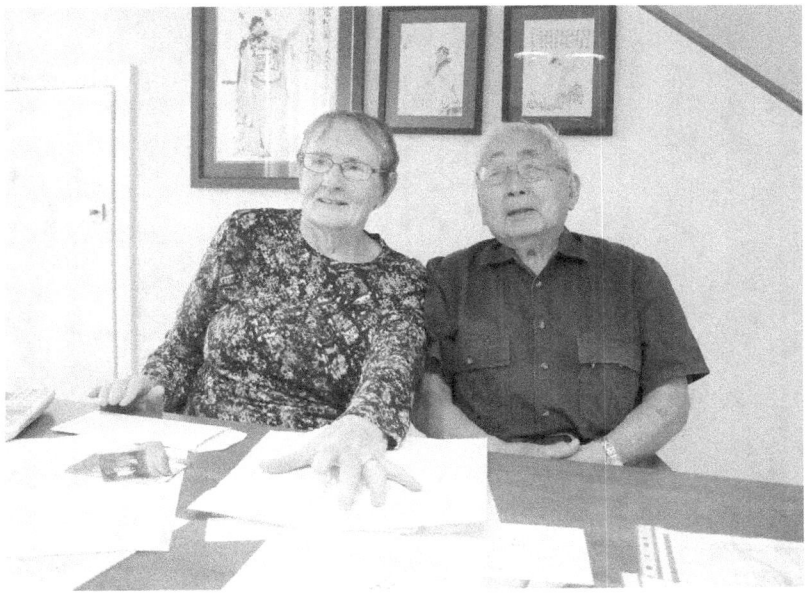

Figure 1.2 Nancy and William Lee in Sydney in 2017.

The Gay family's market garden

George Louis Gay (1870–1946) was born in Zhongshan's Du Tou village (Figure 1.3). He left there for Australia in 1890. In the first decade of the 20th century, he managed a banana plantation in Fiji for the Wing On company that had been founded by a partnership of fellow-Zhongshanese based in Sydney's Haymarket. On his return to Australia, he married Ada Hong (a Chinese–Australian woman from Goulburn) and they acquired the lease on a block of land in Rose Bay, a salubrious suburb on Sydney Harbour, where they established a market garden. When the local council resumed the land in the 1920s for what would become the Royal Sydney Golf Club, the Gay family began market gardening on 23 acres they bought at Guildford, 20 kilometres northwest of the Sydney CBD. By this time they had five of what would become an eight-child family, all of whom in one way or another contributed their labour to the garden's success.

The Lees and the Gays pursued two different migration strategies in Australia, retailing and market gardening, each of them mainstays of the Chinese migrant economy there prior to World War II. Both helped shape the cultural landscape of Australia's cities and country towns. By the 1880s in New South Wales, white Australians had to a significant extent become dependent on Chinese market gardens for fresh vegetables and fruit (Beattie 2007). In 1885, there were 54 Chinese market gardens in Sydney alone (J. Fitzgerald 2007:

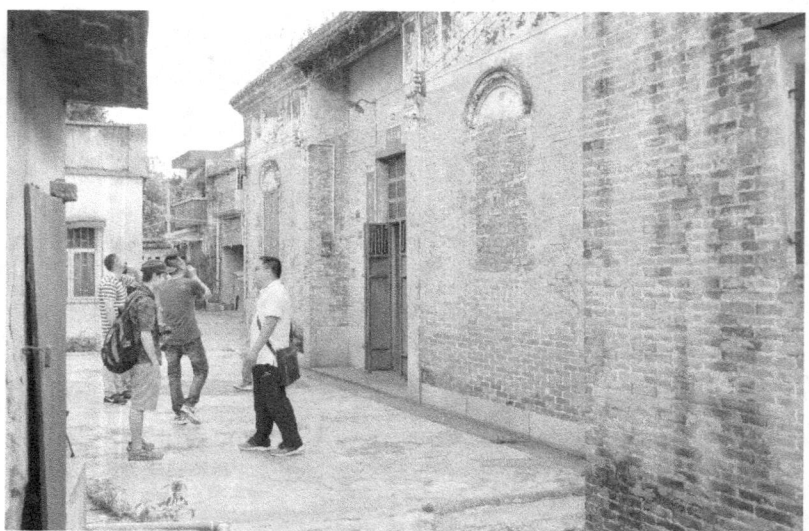

Figure 1.3 The ancestral house of George Louis Gay, Du Tou village, Zhongshan.

122), the sites of some of which are now listed on the NSW government's heritage register.[5] The great majority of Chinese who went overseas in the 19th century had been farmers before leaving their home counties, and it can be said of many of them that they escaped the labour of the fields in China only to find themselves tilling the soil of California (Tsu 2013) or New South Wales (McGowan 2005). But the horticultural knowledge and skills brought with them from China – crucially in rain-poor Australia, this included irrigation skills – allowed them to carve out a niche in the local economy (Boileau 2017).

The land acquired by George Gay and Ada Hong at Guildford in Sydney in the 1920s came with a timber bungalow that had French doors opening onto a verandah around three of its sides. However, much of the land was bush-covered and had to be cleared before they could begin growing the crops of lettuce, potatoes and other vegetables they would sell at a shared stall at the fruit and vegetable market in Chinatown, transporting them there first by horse and cart and later in a truck they purchased. During the Great Depression of the 1930s, the family lived largely off the land, eating their own vegetables and the eggs laid by their own hens.

Testifying to the strength of ties between Australia and Zhongshan in the pre-war years, in the 1930s, George and Ada Gay sent their son, Bill, to school in Zhongshan for three years. This was despite George having put down roots in Australia and Ada Gay having been born in the country. Before returning to Sydney when he was 17, Bill married a Zhongshan girl, Rosina, who accompanied him back to Sydney where they lived and worked on the market garden. When war broke out in 1939, market gardening was deemed an essential industry by the government, meaning that Bill Gay and his brothers were exempt from military service. The garden kept operating till the 1950s when the land was bought by the local government and turned into a park. A plaque erected there by the local government commemorates the market garden and the generosity of the Gay family during the 1930s when the vegetables they donated helped their Anglo-Australian neighbours survive the Great Depression.

Tim Jang

On a morning in December 2017, my colleagues and I were invited to visit Zheng Si Hong and her husband Gao Wei Teng in the Zhongshan village of Pang Tou. They lived in a small two-storey flat-roofed house with a balcony overlooking the street, a modern house whose brick walls were covered with cement stucco and surfaced with pale blue mosaic tiles speckled with brown (Figure 1.4). It was very much the style of house constructed in the decade or so after 1978 when millions of people across China rushed to build new houses or renovate existing ones after a long period, beginning in the 1940s, when virtually no new houses were built. More houses

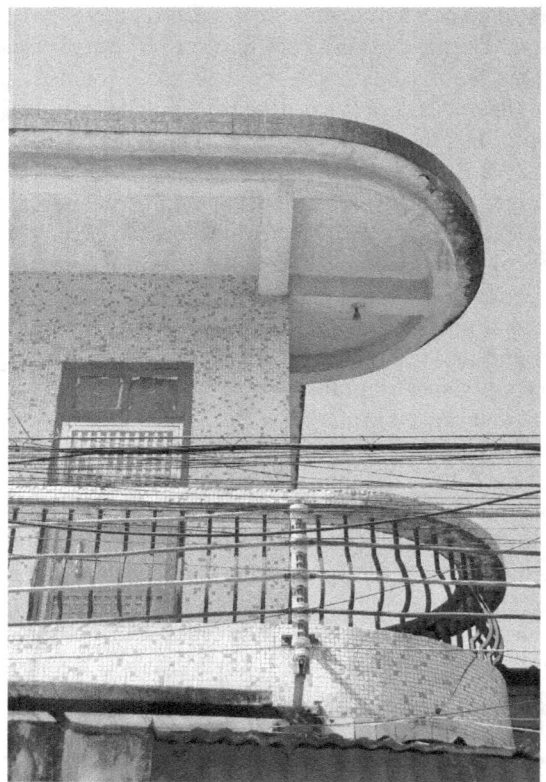

Figure 1.4 The upper floor that was added in the 1990s to the house built by
Tim Jang in Pang Tou village, c. 1910s.

are estimated to have been built in China in the years 1979 to 1985 than
in the previous three decades (Knapp and Shen 1992: 63). What the col-
ourfully modern façade of this house concealed, however, was an older
single-storey dwelling that Si Hong's grandfather, Tim Jang, had commissioned in the early 20th century with money sent home from Queensland,
Australia, where he had gone in 1898 at the age of 17, planning to search
for gold. The older house is 'stratified' within the newer one: a heavy
wooden door belonging to the original house remains in place between the
kitchen and a back room; wooden beams that supported the roof of the old
single-storey house now support the floor of the added upper storey.

In Pang Tou that morning in 2017, over numerous rounds of tea served in
tiny bowls, Si Hong related the story of her grandfather's life in Australia,
as far as she had managed to piece it together, and the story of her search

for his grave. The dying wish of her own father had been that the grave be found and that an offering be made there to Tim Jang's spirit. Si Hong told us she had been haunted by the thought that her grandfather had laboured in Australia to make a better life for his family in China but in the end had died alone, far from home.[6]

Tim Jang's destination in 1898 had been Cooktown in tropical north Queensland but upon his arrival there he found the Queensland gold rush that had begun in 1873 was over. He chose to move south to Gordonvale, a small town about 28 kilometres south of Cairns, where he took up market gardening, growing potatoes, beans, lettuce and other vegetables. He lived in a shed-like structure in the garden and sold his produce around the streets of Gordonvale from his horse and dray (Chan 2015: 16). Eventually, he made enough money to own a greengrocer shop in town but lost it during the 1930s Depression. He lived thereafter in his market garden.

On a visit home to Zhongshan in 1911, when he was 30, Tim Jang married Jang Low She and the following year their first daughter was born. He fathered a child on each of his following visits to Zhongshan. In 1926, his second daughter was born and 1928 saw the birth of his son, Jang Gock Si, who would be Si Hong's father. Tim Jang's final visit home was in 1932 – he had wanted his only son to accompany him back to Australia, but the boy had not wanted to leave his mother. He continued sending money back to Zhongshan, remitting a large sum in 1951 which his son collected in Hong Kong (Chan 2015: 16). Tim Jang died on 25 May 1952 at Cairns Base Hospital at the age of 71 after a long period of illness.

On his visits to Pang Tou village, Tim Jang carried with him from Australia camphorwood chests packed with objects that included Akubra brand hats (commonly worn by Australian farmers), oil lamps and tools, some of which remain in the possession of Zhang Si Hong's family (Chan 2015: 16). During our 2017 visit, I examined some of the tools, which included two wood planes manufactured by Tertius Keen & Co of Glascow, an Australian-made Eureka brand cold chisel, wooden-handled files and a bit-braced hand drill (Figure 1.5). Jumbled together in a cardboard carton, the metal components of the tools were covered with a thin patina of rust but were otherwise quite serviceable. It is possible the tools were used in the building of the house that Tim Jang financed and perhaps worked on during his visits.

The material heritage of Tim Jang's life as a migrant consists of a transnationally distributed assemblage of objects and sites that include the house in Pang Tou village, the site of the market garden in Queensland (the hut is no longer standing but the location of the garden is known), the carton of tools and the camphorwood chests that survive in his ancestral village and finally his grave in a Cairns cemetery. This assemblage has its counterpart in those others that span the myriad of migration corridors globally, populating them with objects that must number in the millions. In the emigrant villages

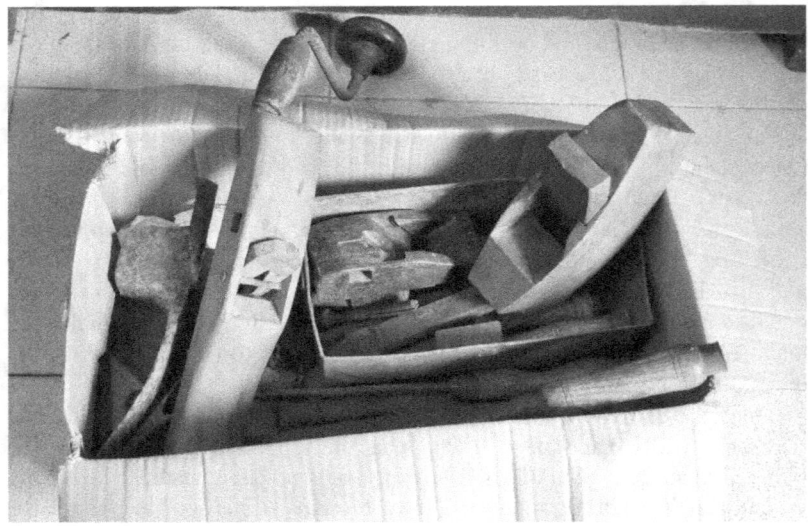

Figure 1.5 A box of tools brought to Pang Tou village by Tim Jang.

of Zhongshan, they included, in addition to the things Tim Jang carried with him, bicycles and Singer sewing machines. At the other end of the migration corridor, in places such as Sydney, they included imported Chinese ceramics (e.g., jars for preserved ginger), abacuses, statues of gods and gardening implements. For Voss et al. (2018: 415), such objects suggest

> the use of material culture to create a "home away from home." Whether migrants were engaging in the mundane task of grating vegetables, eating meals, or lighting ritual oil lamps, these objects provided them with visual, tactile, and haptic continuity in new social and physical environments.

In 2008, Zheng Si Hong set off for Australia with her husband in the hope of fulfilling her father's wish that Tim Jang's grave be located. They failed to find any trace of Tim Jang on that visit but returned in 2015 when, with the aid of a group of local Chinese historians in Cairns, they found the site of his market garden along with the building housing his former grocery shop, and his unmarked grave. They installed a headstone on the grave with a plaque containing an epitaph in Chinese characters; they offered incense and prayers to Tim Jang's spirit. For Zheng Si Hong, it was not enough to know her grandfather had a life in Australia, she wanted to visit the landscape of his life there and the site of his grave. Like thousands of migrant descendants globally, she was engaged in the kind of heritage-making project in which 'being there' is crucial.

A 40-year lacuna

Whatever the precise reasons for Tim Jang's failure to travel back to Zhongshan in the years between his visit in 1932 and his death in 1952, they are likely to relate at least in part to the lacuna in travel along the China–Australia migration corridor, mentioned earlier, that began with the Japanese invasion of his homeland in 1938 and did not really end until the beginning of the Reform Era in 1978. There was, admittedly, some movement along the corridor between the end of the Pacific War in 1945 and the founding of the PRC in 1949 and even during the Mao Era, but travel was difficult and conditions on the mainland were unstable and at certain times dangerous for returnees. Kourelis (2020) describes a somewhat similar lacuna in contact between Greek Americans and their home villages during and after World War II (between the 1940 German invasion of Greece and the end of the 1946–1949 Greek Civil War). During that time, many of the relatives of Greek migrants were killed and whole emigrant villages were erased from the landscape. In Zhongshan, by contrast, the pre-1940s built environment of the emigrant villages is remarkably intact.

It was a different story for the relatives of overseas Chinese living in the Pearl River Delta region, many of whom died at the hands of the Japanese and some others were killed during the Land Reform years of the 1950s after being classified as members of the reviled landlord class. The levelling effect of communist social and economic reforms in the 1950s meant that the families of overseas Chinese who had become relatively prosperous from having male members earning money overseas lost all that wealth, including their land and houses. The impact of the war and especially of subsequent Maoist policies created a profound break in the way the Chinese diaspora historicised their homeland ties. The period prior to these events was rendered a 'before' time, its counterpart 'after' being marked by the 1978 beginning of the Reform Era and China's reopening to the world.

At a village level, very little building construction occurred during the lacuna in transnational flows. In rural areas, during the 1950s and 1960s, the People's Communes repurposed existing ancestral halls and temples as communal dining halls and administrative offices. Very few new houses were built and many of the large houses built by emigrants in their home villages were appropriated as housing for multiple families. The hiatus in housing construction meant that most of the earlier migrant-built houses survived into the 1980s and beyond.

Stanley Hunt's return to Mashan

The four-decade lacuna helped shape the life of Stanley Hunt (1927–2019). When in the latter part of his life he turned his energies and wealth to building a school in his ancestral village, he was revitalising a tradition of education philanthropy among overseas Chinese that had been long suspended (Cheng 2020). Stanley Hunt (birth name, Chan Pui-Tak) was born in Zhongshan in 1927 and migrated to Australia in 1939 with his mother and two younger siblings, fleeing the Japanese who had invaded Guangdong the year before. They joined Stanley's father who had been in Australia for some years and who at the time of their arrival was operating a general store at Warialda, a small town in northern New South Wales, population 1,025. The information presented here comes from an interview conducted with Stanley in October 2017 and from his autobiography, *From Shekki to Sydney* (Hunt 2009).

Stanley adapted well to life in Warialda. In his book, he describes life as a teenager there: delivering groceries on a bicycle, making and flying Chinese-style kites and selling some of them from the shop, and driving a horse and cart around the surrounding towns to sell the vegetables the family grew in a market garden they acquired. He learned English after school hours from a nun at the Catholic school. It was in 1945, by which time Stanley had six siblings, that his parents decided to move to Sydney and once there bought a fruit and vegetable shop in the city's western suburbs, moving into the three-bedroom flat above the shop. The business did so well that after a year they acquired another such shop, in the nearby suburb of Auburn, which was given over to Stanley to run and which he quickly built up to the point that he was employing 28 people, Chinese and Anglo-Australian, to help run it. In 1948, he married Valmai Tuck-Lee; together they would have four children.

Stanley found he had a talent for attracting and retaining customers. In 1956, he opened 'Stanley's Gift Store,' also in Auburn, and by 1960 he expanded into the motel business. Although he belonged to the Chungshan Society in Sydney, the association for migrants from Zhongshan and their descendants, it was not until 1979 that he actually revisited Zhongshan for the first time. He and Valmai were on a group tour and were unable to visit his ancestral village, Mashan, but he did so on a trip he made the following year with Valmai and his father. While strolling around the edge of the village, he came upon a boy herding pigs and ducks and he asked him why he was not at school.

> I said to him, 'How come. Chairman Mao said no child will go without school.' He said, 'We don't have any classroom.' So I decided to build a school for them.[7]

The two-storey classroom block of the new Mashan school opened in 1983, named the Sung-Sun Hall of Learning after Stanley's father (Figure 1.6). From 1979 almost until his death in July 2019, Stanley revisited Mashan every year, overseeing a series of additions to the school, which he and his siblings were funding: a school library that was opened in 1985, named after their mother, and later a sealed running track and a residential block for teachers.

It seems significant to me that Stanley Hunt's first visit to his father's village, 40 years after leaving Zhongshan, triggered a 'futuring' project rather than a conservation one. He had no interest in restoring his small ancestral house, the interior of which had been colonised by weeds after its roof fell in. Instead, he built a new house for his father's sister who had remained in the village and then directed his money and energy to the education of Mashan's new generation. One might think that in building the school and naming it after his parents, Stanley was establishing what would become his material legacy in Mashan. But in 2020 the classroom block was demolished after it was found not to comply with new national standards for earthquake resistance. In response to this and to a rapid growth in student enrolments, a much larger classroom block was erected by the government in 2012 on the elevated ground immediately behind the block

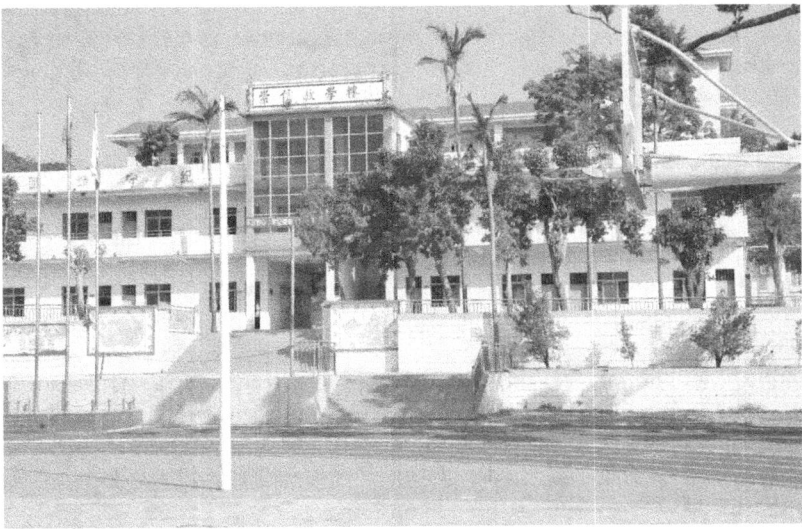

Figure 1.6 The 1983 classroom block at Mashan school, built by Stanley Hunt. This 2017 photograph shows the exterior as renovated in the 2000s.

Stanley built. Visiting the school in 2017, I was struck by the way the new classroom block dominated the school site, leaving the original and soon to be demolished building looking diminutive and overtaken, despite it being only 34 years old. The fate of Stanley's building is representative of what has happened to many thousands of buildings erected in the Reform Era (beginning 1978), only to be abandoned and demolished a few decades later, deemed obsolete, dangerous or simply unfashionable. This has led to the lifespan of buildings in China being only 35 years on average and commonly only 20 years, well under half the building turnover rate of the USA and Europe.[8]

Walking in 2017 through the original classroom block prompted reflections on its archaeological character. The building was an eloquent testament to China's economic state in the early 1980s, still in the aftermath of the Cultural Revolution. Stanley had struggled to assemble building materials for the school at a time when there was an acute shortage of cement and steel reinforcing bars (rebar) for concrete. The building ended up embodying those shortages, the poor quality of its concrete construction leading to its later failure to meet seismic resistance standards and hence to its demolition. The inability to source readymade blackboards for the classrooms meant 'blackboards' were painted directly onto the walls using matt black paint (Figure 1.7). Later, aluminium-framed blackboards were screwed onto the walls over the old 'blackboards'. At some point in the brief life of the building, electric wiring in PVC pipes had been laid across the surfaces of walls for new light switches, power points and ceiling fans. This layering, or stratification, of the new onto the old was also to be seen on the building's exterior in the form of a veneer of white ceramic tiles that had been laid over the original surface of cement render.

These additions to the building had been funded by Stanley Hunt as he strove to keep it from becoming anachronistic. The building, as well as being part of the built heritage of China's Reform Era, was also at some level part of Stanley's personal heritage, although when interviewed in 2017 he gave no indication of being dismayed by its ephemerality. Loss, in this respect, can be a diminishment but also 'generative and emancipatory' (DeSilvey and Harrison 2020: 3). Stanley's legacy, I suggest, reposed not in the school itself but in the learning acquired by the schools' students and how that learning has rippled through their future and the future of Mashan. The demolition of Stanley's classroom block has opened up space for new school facilities currently under construction – the dissolution of the old is enfolded in the assembling of the new.

When the students and teachers moved from the old classroom block into the new one behind it, they left behind the old desks, rusted ceiling

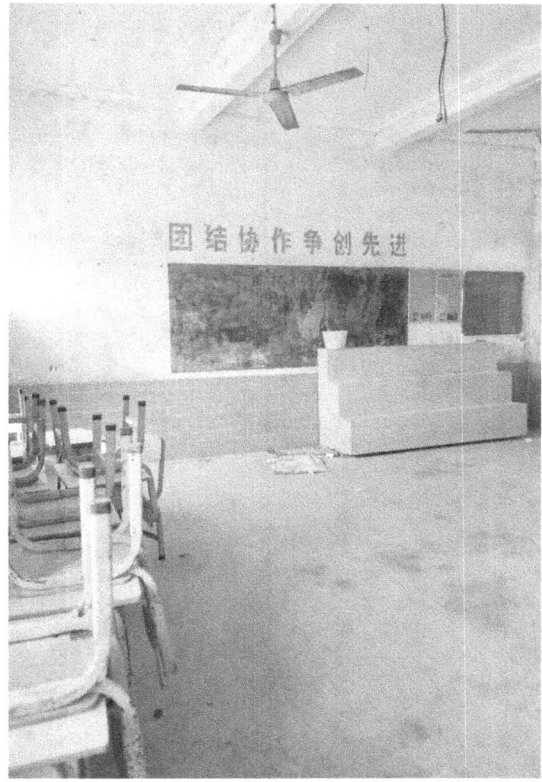

Figure 1.7 A classroom in the abandoned classroom block of Mashan school.

fans, faded pictures of socialist heroes on the walls and chalk-written rows of Chinese characters on the blackboards. Dust accumulated and in some rooms flakes of white paint fell from the walls and ceilings to lie on unswept floors. And then, with Stanley Hunt's death in 2019, the life force that had driven the building's construction and sustained its renovations finally expired, a year or so before his classroom block's demolition.[9]

The school on the edge of Mashan village had been a building project of transnational scope. Stanley's shops and motels in Sydney generated the wealth that allowed him to begin building the school. And this first act of building entailed him in an ongoing series of related acts of construction and renovation, necessitating a rhythm of annual journeys to and fro across the Zhongshan–Australia migration corridor. It is in this sense, for example, that the heritage corridor concept takes on substance.

Notes

1 In Australia, since the 1990s, there has been a surge of historical research on the transnational dimension of the Chinese migrant experience. See, for example, Deacon, Russell and Woollacott 2008, J. Fitzgerald 2007, Loy-Wilson 2014, Walker and Sobocinska 2012, and Williams 2018. This research includes attention to circular patterns of travel between Australia, China and Southeast Asia and to regional webs of kin ties and trade.
2 See Kate Bagnall's blog, *The Tiger's Mouth: Thoughts on the History and Heritage of Chinese Australia* http://chineseaustralia.org
3 Tim Jang's granddaughter, Zheng Si Hong, was assisted in her research by members of the Cairns and District Chinese Association in Queensland (Chan 2015).
4 For a global history of anti-Asian immigration restrictions, see McKeown (2001).
5 For heritage listings of Chinese market gardens in Sydney, see www.environment.nsw.gov.au/heritageapp/ViewHeritageItemDetails.aspx?ID=5044696
6 Information on Tim Jang's life in Australia has been drawn from the 2017 interview with Zheng Si Hong and from an unpublished paper by Lai Chu Chan (2015).
7 Interview with Stanley Hunt, October 2017, Sydney.
8 'How will a slowing China cope with rapidly aging buildings,' *China Economic Review*, 28 June, 2013. https://chinaeconomicreview.com/unstable-foundations-part-2/
9 The school library, opened in 1985 and named for Stanley's mother, as well as the running track and the residential block for teachers, all remain in place.

References

Bagnall, Kate. 2012. 'Crossing oceans and cultures,' in D. Walker and A. Sobocinska (eds.), *Australia's Asia: From Yellow Peril to Asian Century*, pp. 121–144. Perth: University of Western Australia Publishing.

Bagnall, Kate. 2013. 'Landscapes of memory and forgetting: Indigo and Shek Quey Lee,' *Chinese Southern Diaspora Studies* 6: 7–24.

Beattie, James. 2007. 'Growing Chinese influences in New Zealand: Chinese gardens, identity and meaning,' *New Zealand Journal of Asian Studies* 9(1): 38–61.

Boccagni, Paolo. 2014. 'What's in a (migrant) house? Changing domestic spaces, the negotiation of belonging and home-making in Ecuadorian migration,' *Housing Theory and Society* 31(3): 277–293, https://doi.org/10.1080/14036096.2013.867280.

Boccagni, Paolo and Marta Bivand Erdal. 2020. 'On the theoretical potential of "remittance houses": Towards a research agenda across emigration contexts,' *Journal of Ethnic and Migration Studies*, published online, https://doi.org/10.1080/1369183X.2020.1804340.

Boileau, Joanna. 2017. *Chinese Market Gardens in Australia and New Zealand: Gardens of Prosperity*. London: Palgrave Macmillan.

Chan, Lai Chu. 2015. 'Jang Tim: Father, grandfather, greengrocer,' unpublished paper, Cairns and District Chinese Association Inc.

Cheng, Christopher. 2020. 'Beacons of modern learning: Diaspora-funded schools in the China-Australia corridor,' *Asian and Pacific Migration Journal* 29(2): 139–162, https://doi.org/10.1177/0117196820930309.

Deacon, Desley, Penny Russell and Angela Woollacott (eds.). 2008. *Transnational Ties: Australian Lives in the World*. Canberra: Australian National University E Press.

DeSilvey, Caitlin and Harrison, Rodney. 2020. 'Anticipating loss: Rethinking endangerment in heritage futures,' *International Journal of Heritage Studies* 26(1): 1–7, https://doi.org/10.1080/13527258.2019.1644530.

Fitzgerald, John. 2007. *Big White Lie: Chinese Australians in White Australia*. Sydney: University of New South Wales Press.

Fitzgerald, Shirley. 2007. *Red Tape, Gold Scissors: The Story of Sydney's Chinese*. Sydney: Halstead.

Hsu, Madeline Y. 2000. *Dreaming of Gold, Dreaming of Home: Transnationalism and Migration Between the United States and South China 1882–1943*. Stanford: Stanford University Press.

Hunt, Stanley. 2009. *From Shekki to Sydney*. Sydney: Wild Peony.

Ingold, Tim. 2007. *Lines: A Brief History*. London: Routledge.

Ingold, Tim. 2011. *Being Alive: Essays on Movement, Knowledge and Description*. Abingdon, UK: Routledge.

Knapp, Ronald G. and Shen Dongqi. 1992. 'Changing village landscapes,' in Ronald G. Knapp (ed.), *Chinese Landscapes: The Village as Place*, pp. 47–72. Honolulu: University of Hawaii Press.

Kourelis, Kostis. 2020. 'Three Elenis: Archaeologies of the Greek American home,' *Journal of Modern Greek Studies* 38: 85–108, https://doi.org/10.1353/mgs.2020.0005.

Loy-Wilson, Sophie. 2014. 'A Chinese shopkeeper on the Atherton Tablelands: Tracing connections between regional Queensland and regional China in Taam Szu Pui's *My life and work*,' *Queensland Review* 21(2): 160–176, https://doi.org/10.1017/qre.2014.23.

McGowan, Barry. 2005. 'Chinese market gardens in southern and western New South Wales,' *Australian Humanities Review* 23, online publication, http://australianhumanitiesreview.org/2005/07/01/chinese-market-gardens-in-southern-and-western-new-south-wales/

McKeown, Adam. 2001. *Chinese Migrant Networks and Cultural Change: Peru, Chicago, Hawaii, 1900–1936*. Chicago: University of Chicago Press.

Tsu, Cecilia, M. 2013. *Garden of the World: Asian Immigrants and the Making of Agriculture in California's Santa Clara Valley*. Oxford: Oxford University Press, https://doi.org/10.1093/acprof:oso/9780199734771.001.0001.

Voss, Barbara L, J. Ryan Kennedy, Jinhua (Selia) Tan and Laura W. Ng. 2018. 'The archaeology of home: *Qiaoxiang* and nonstate actors in the archaeology of the Chinese diaspora,' *American Antiquity* 83(3): 407–426.

Walker, David and Agnieszka Sobocinska. 2012. *Australia's Asia: From Yellow Peril to Asian Century*. Perth: University of Western Australia Press.

Williams, Michael. 2018. *Returning Home with Glory: Chinese Villagers Around the Pacific, 1849 to 1949*. Hong Kong: Hong Kong University Press.

Yeoh, Brenda S.A. 1996. *Contesting Space in Colonial Singapore: Power Relations and the Urban Built Environment*. Singapore: Singapore University Press.

Yu, Henry. 2011. 'Intermittent rhythms of the Cantonese Pacific,' in D. R. Gabaccia and D. Hoerder (eds.), *Connecting Seas and Connecting Ocean Rims: Indian, Atlantic, and Pacific Oceans and China Seas Migrations from the 1830s to the 1930s*, pp. 393–414. Leiden: Brill.

2 The distributed materiality of migration

Distributed personhood and agency in the heritage corridor

Central to the concept of the 'heritage corridor' (Byrne 2016), with its context in the history of transnational migration, is the idea that the built environment of migrants is stretched between their origin and destination locales and that it emerges out of the agency of people and objects in collectives that are themselves transnationally distributed. Thus, the kind of corridor I have in mind throughout this book is not a space in which people, objects and money simply move along in both directions. It is a space in which the lives of people at either end – those who leave and those they leave behind – are coloured to a greater or lesser extent by the phenomenon of transnational simultaneity (Levitt and Glick Schiller 2004; Tsuda 2012) and by what Ien Ang (2011: 86) refers to as a 'diasporic state of mind' that arises from the interplay of long-distance memories, attachments and senses of belonging, a state of mind in which migrants commonly experience home and away simultaneously.

As Nick Enfield (2017: 9) points out,

> It is easy to think that "an agent" should coincide exactly with an individual. But this is seldom, if ever, the case. One reason agents do not equal individuals is that the elements of agency can be divided up and shared out by multiple people in relation to a single course of action.

This is not so much a matter of dividing up tasks among individuals – for example, between the Zhongshan migrant in Sydney who earns the money to build a house in his or her home village in Zhongshan and the relatives there who oversee its construction. The agency of each of the individuals involved in the house-building project is essentially relational; it is enmeshed in the agency not only of the other people involved but of the

DOI: 10.4324/9781003088714-3

particular capacities of the objects and materials that are also involved in the project. Focusing for the moment on the human element, this vision of transnationally distributed agency draws on Marilyn Strathern's (1988) concept of the 'dividual', in which personhood is never unitary, it is comprised of a complex of relations between humans and nonhumans. In this way, personhood is a 'distributed' phenomenon, after Alfred Gell's (1998) proposition that the kind of social agency possessed by inanimate art objects means they can be thought of as elements of the 'distributed personhood' of artists, art collectors and others involved in the art world.

The work carried out by local carpenters, craftsmen and building labourers on the new house in the village is symmetrical with and dependent upon the labour expended by migrants in their overseas setting, which, converted into remittance funds, pays for its construction. Remittances are a crystallisation of the sender's labour (Sandell 2010: 194). The sender's productivity abroad translates into productivity at home and the product in question, the 'remittance house' serves as a placeholder in the village for absent migrants, affording them an 'absent presence' there.[1] This is important from a heritage point of view in that it points to what for many migrants is a translocal sense of belonging. As Steve Taylor writes of Punjabi migrants in Britain, even though they have put down roots there, they insist on the need to maintain houses in their home villages on 'land that should never be sold' (2015: 199), impelled to do so because the land and houses 'signify enfranchisement to a particular home and identity' (2015: 200).

Turning to the nonhuman agents involved in the emergence of a remittance house, the perspective offered here is one not so much of migrants having material assets distributed across a migration corridor but of them being intimately entangled in an 'object world' of transnational scope.[2] The remittance house, for example, is not a passive possession of the emigrant. As Julie Chu (2010) observes of remittance houses in the Fujian village she studies, they are capable of provoking feelings of both pride and embarrassment in their owners and occupiers that impel them on particular courses of action. Boccagni and Murcia (2021: 61) also acknowledge the agentic capacity of the remittance house, as manifest in 'the practical, relational, and emotional work required by their maintenance – indeed, by their very existence.'

To regard the material fabric of the houses as an active participant in the remittance house 'assemblage' (DeLanda 2016; Latour 1993) is to go against the Cartesian ontology that disposes us to think of villages and houses as objects whose existence is separate from that of their human inhabitants. This is the 'modernist charade' wherein inanimate objects occupy a separate space to intentional human subjects (Witmore 2014). The existential phenomenology of thinkers such as Martin Heidegger and Maurice Merleau-Ponty counters this charade, allowing us to see such objects as at once extensions of our embodied selves into external matter and extensions of external matter into us (Ahmed 2006: 162). Merleau-Ponty, after Leibniz, conceived the interface between our bodies and the external world as pleated or folded (Coole 2010), a conception expressed in Ingold's (2008: 1797) account of an organism's environment as not simply surrounding it but also constituting a 'zone of entanglement' around it. In the case of remittance houses, this zone is transnational in scope.

The two sections that follow provide an overview of the phenomenon of remittance building in a contemporary as well as historical setting, with an eye to its implications for the heritage record of migration. Discussion then moves to a more intimate register as the emotional and affective dimensions of migrant material assemblages are considered.

Heritage in the remittance landscape

The term 'heritage corridor' takes its inspiration from 'remittance corridor', a term commonly used in the banking world. While in this book I am interested in the heritage of migration at both ends of the corridor, here the focus of attention will be on that which emerges in the migrant's origin place, such as in the emigrant villages of migrant-sending countries.

The significance of remittances to the global economy is immense, total global remittance flows reaching USD 554 billion in 2019 (projected to fall to USD 508 billion in 2020 and USD 470 billion in 2021 due to the impact of the coronavirus pandemic).[3] The top five remittance-receiving countries are India, China, Mexico, the Philippines and Egypt, in order of total capital flow. Vertovec (2004: 973) sees the sheer scale of capital movement along remittance corridors as having the capacity to 'modify the value systems and everyday social life of people across entire regions.' While the capital flows were of a smaller scale in the 19th and 20th centuries, they were still sufficient to bring into being a 'remittance landscape' (Lopez 2010) encompassing the origin and destination locales of particular migration corridors, this forming the basis of the 'heritage corridor' concept.

In most cases, the bulk of remitted funds is used to support the relatives of migrants who have remained in the origin place, helping to pay for their subsistence, medical bills, school fees and so on. Nevertheless, and allowing that building costs in the home countries of the Global South are often far lower than in the country where the money is earned, the proportion of remittances spent on building construction has been sufficient to significantly alter the built environment of migrant-sending villages and towns in regions that include Africa, Latin America, the Middle East and Asia

(Lopez 2015; Cohen 2001; Datta 2008; Lozanovska 2019; Miller 2008; Taylor 2015). In turn, given that some countries in these regions have long histories of emigration, a significant part of the built heritage of the Global South consists of buildings paid for by remittances. This is certainly the case for the emigrant counties of the Pearl River Delta.

Ayona Datta (2008: 527) describes as a process of 'productive imagination' the effort that Polish émigrés in London devote to planning the houses they will build back in Poland. In such studies, it is apparent that the acts of anticipating and imagining are as integral to the production of such a house as is the act of carpentry. Also, it is evident that via the exchange of ideas between those at home and those away, these acts coalesce in the form of a distributed imaginary. This would agree with Levitt and Glick Schiller's (2004) thoughts about the role of simultaneity in the experiential reality of migration. Often, the physical distinctiveness of the architecture that emerges from remittance flows sets the recipient villages and towns off from non-emigrant locales in the same regions. Madeline Hsu describes how in Taishan County, in the western part of the Pearl River Delta, new villages sprouted in the 1920s and 1930s beside old ones:

> These new villages consisted of clusters of fifteen to 30 'foreign' houses (*yanglou*), built of oven-fired grey brick and concrete and decorated with Western motifs: stained-glass windows, Greek columns, and porches, as well as bas-relief moldings in plaster and tile. The new houses, built for both comfort and show, sometimes rose to three or four stories, towering over the older houses in the village.
>
> (Hsu 2000, 44–45)

In Zhongshan County, just 60 kilometres or so east of Taishan, migrant-built houses share much of the stylistic vocabulary of those in Taishan while at the same time having an easily recognisable distinctiveness (see Chapter 3). It is apparent that this distinction relates to Zhongshan's closeness to Hong Kong and its susceptibility, as discussed later, to early 20th-century architectural trends there. But it is also likely to reflect the density of human settlement and cultural diversification in the Pearl River Delta region, evidenced, for example, in the fact that Taishan and Zhongshan speak different sub-languages of Cantonese. What this points to is that those 'at home' in this remittance-receiving region had as much say in what was built as their remittance-sending relatives away overseas.

Such was the intensity of new remittance-fuelled building in the emigrant villages of the Pearl River Delta in the early decades of the 20th century that numerous houses and other buildings would have been under construction in any one of them at any one time, some of them taking years to complete, dependent as they were on the incremental flow of remittance funds. They may have resembled in this respect those emigrant villages in parts of today's Global South where many buildings are in an almost permanent state of emergence and incompletion, as symbolised by the steel reinforcing sprouting from their flat concrete roofs. In Mexico, such structures are known as 'castles of hope' (Forty 2012: 40). To focus on architecture alone would, however, be to neglect the immense effect of remittances on health and wellbeing. One indication of this in south China was an increase of between four and five centimetres in human stature in the period between 1850 and 1930 (Ward 2013).

And in regard to the effects of remittance flows on the built environment of southern China, a great many structures other than houses were built wholly or partly with funds provided by migrants. After the collapse of the Qing Dynasty in 1911 and the establishment of the Republican government in 1912, many Chinese migrants in Australia, Canada and the USA, as well as in Southeast Asia and Hong Kong, became enthusiastic contributors to the building of modern schools in their home counties (Cheng 2020; Williams 2018: 82–83), as well as health clinics (Johnson and Woon 1997: 46; Williams 2018: 82). They also invested in the first modern roads, bridges, railroads and bus services (Hsu 2000: 48–49; Williams 2003: 86–87). In some areas, electricity generators and piped water infrastructure were funded by those overseas. Alongside these investments in modernity, most migrants also sent money back for the building of new lineage halls (Woon 1984; Williams 2018: 17) and temples or the rebuilding of old ones. To this extent, remittance houses, which are a key focus of this and the following chapter, sat within a remittance landscape, which, while literally grounded in the local terrain, was simultaneously part of a diasporic material domain in which origin and destination locales, as well as places in between, were elements of a material continuum.

As proposed earlier, this remittance landscape took form in the context of transborder networks and assemblages involving globally dispersed actors. For all the concrete solidity and material heft of the buildings financed by overseas Chinese, and for all that their foundations are sunk in the soil of the local terrain, these buildings are constituted in assemblages of transnational scope – as heritage objects, they simply do not make sense in isolation from these assemblages.

'Sterling houses' in San Tin

A localised insight into the effect of overseas migration on an emigrant village can be found in the case of San Tin, a single-lineage village located in the north-western corner of the New Territories of Hong Kong. James

Watson's (1975) landmark ethnography describes how, beginning in the 1950s, San Tin became the origin node of a global diaspora. Established in the 14th century by the founder of the Man lineage, Man Sai-go, who had migrated from elsewhere in Guangdong, San Tin's economy was based on rice grown in fields reclaimed from the mudflats of Deep Bay and marketed in the area of Shenzhen, just five or so kilometres to the north, which after 1898 would lie on the China side of the China–Hong Kong border.[4] But the closure of the border in the 1950s left this economy in crisis, provoking the Mans to switch to an emigrant economy. San Tin's origin as a village stemmed from Man Sai-go's willingness to migrate; its survival five centuries later depended on his descendants making the same choice.

At the time of his fieldwork in the late 1960s, Watson found that 87 percent of the working-age males of San Tin were residing in London and Amsterdam (with a lesser presence in a few other centres), some of them owning Chinese restaurants, others working in the kitchens of those restaurants. Man lineage emigrants remitted most of their wages back to San Tin where a significant proportion was used to construct new houses, known locally as 'sterling houses' because they were mostly built with pounds sterling. Constructed of reinforced concrete, these two-storey structures with their flat roofs, cantilevered balconies, steel-frame windows and plain stucco-cement rendered walls were strikingly different from the older, single-storey houses of the village, which had traditional tiled, gabled roofs (Figure 2.1). By the 1980s, a newer generation of remittance houses was being constructed in San Tin, including some rising to three or four storeys, their exterior walls and balconies surfaced with ceramic tiles, often in pastel colours. A decade or so later, the trend was towards brown and gold tiles, these dwellings coming to be known as 'Spanish' houses (Figure 2.2).

The sterling houses of San Tin that are extant today, given their association with the crisis which the Man lineage underwent and survived in the late 1950s, could certainly be regarded as heritage sites. But which country's heritage are they? The notion that England could claim some of them as its heritage is not as preposterous as it may seem: the money for them was earned in England, they were envisaged and planned in the kitchens of London restaurants, and many of the builders' descendants are now UK citizens (Watson 2004). An equally strong case could, of course, be made that they belong to the heritage of Hong Kong. If England's claim were to be validated by some hypothetical international heritage disputes tribunal, then by the same token the Man lineage's Chinese restaurants in London could be counter-claimed under Hong Kong's Antiquities and Monuments Ordinance. But this is beside the point: the sterling houses of San Tin are best thought of as residing in transnational space. McKeown's (2001: 75) description of the 19th-century emigrant village in southern China as a 'transnational entity' is apt for a situation in which the lineage estate was

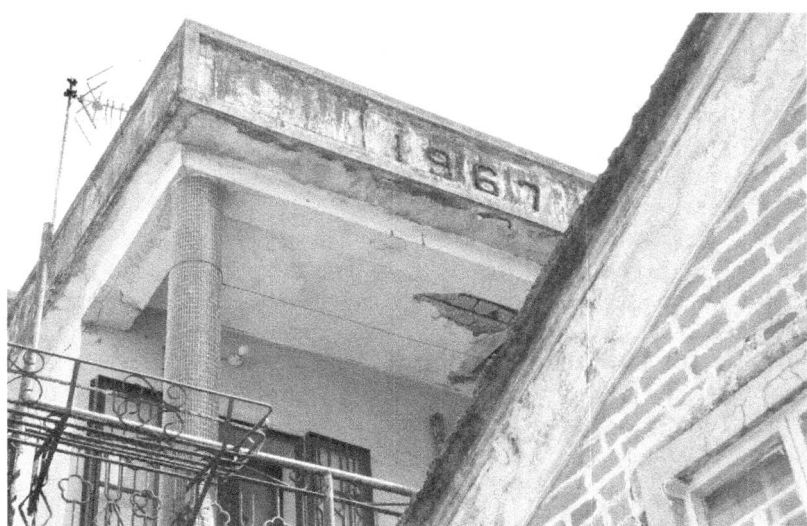

Figure 2.1 A 'sterling house' in San Tin, New Territories, Hong Kong (with date inscription, 1967). The concrete frame house stands immediately behind a traditional brick house with gabled roof.

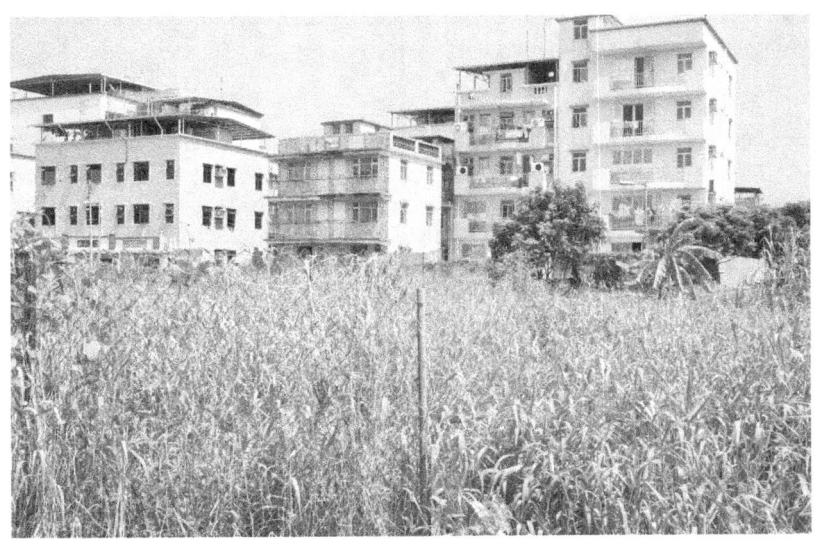

Figure 2.2 A cluster of 'Spanish' houses on the edge of San Tin, New Territories, Hong Kong. In the foreground are fields reclaimed from Deep Bay by the Man lineage.

considered to be uncompromised by the spatial dispersion of its members; keeping the estate intact and in place could at times actually *require* dispersion in the form of internal and transnational migration (Kuhn 2008: 15; Chu 2010: 219).

An irony of the effort devoted by Pearl River Delta emigrants, such as those from San Tin, to building new houses in their home villages is that in many cases they never lived in them, except on occasional visits home. This was the case with most of those built in San Tin. The houses served as placeholders, or proxies, for absent villagers. As Watson (1975, 2004) has shown, they helped anchor the emigrant in the village after it had become the central social and religious node of a transnational network of clan members. Although in the early decades of emigration, investment in the new houses supported what Daniel Miller (2008: 407) calls the 'myth of return', later, when permanent return was no longer an ambition of most, they took on a more symbolic status as statements of belonging to a clan that emigration had deterritorialised.

Migrancy and the affective in-between

Accepting that we experience old things and places by way of sense, affect and emotion, at least as much as by an intellectual apprehension of them, our attachment to them can be expected to accrue at least as much from our histories of embodied experience with them as from deliberative thought. The well-known definition of affect coined by Gregory Seigworth and Melissa Gregg is worth citing here.

> Affect arises in the midst of in-between-ness: in the capacities to act and be acted upon. Affect is an impingement or extrusion of a momentary or sometimes more sustained state of relation *as well as* the passage (and duration of passage) of forces or intensities. That is, affect is found in those intensities that pass body to body (human, non-human, part-body, and otherwise), in those resonances that circulate about, between, and sometimes stick to bodies and worlds.
>
> (Seigworth and Gregg 2010: 1)

The kind of in-betweenness referred to here holds good over a larger space-time scale than those very intimate and immediate settings in which affect is mostly seen to be situated. In the migration context, we might think of it as a body-mind state of being involving intimate relations with transnationally dispersed things. It is in the play of the intensities of affect and emotion across time and space and their enfoldment in the built environment that the notion of a migration heritage corridor gains coherence.

In a study of the ways that recent migrants from Lebanon related to a national park in suburban Sydney, it was found to be impossible to describe this relationality purely as occurring *in* Sydney (Byrne and Goodall 2013). Take, for example, the act of fishing at the edge of the river that flows through the park. For Lebanese immigrant fishers, the specific weight of the Lebanese fishing rod they hold in their hands is precisely the same as those rods they fished with back home, back then. Also the same, or very similar, are the repetitive motions involved in baiting the hook, casting out the line and hauling it in (Goodall et al. 2009: 183). What gives the rod its *affective* weight is a combination of one's personal history of holding similar rods in Lebanon, the propensity of one's body to remember the sensations which go with that and the 'vibrancy' (Bennett 2010) of the matter constituting the rod. Objects are known to play an active role in triggering 'embodied memories' (Connerton 1989) and through the histories we have with them they are liable to become 'sticky' with affect (Ahmed 2010: 35).

Returning to the remittance houses of southern China, I now look more closely at their position in the transnational social field of migration, understanding them to be flexible and permeable entities coextensive with their transnationally stretched community of builders and occupiers. This depiction is consonant with the symmetry of human–nonhuman relations argued for by Latour (1993) and the non-hierarchical positioning of humans in Bryant's (2011) 'flat ontology'. Julie Chu's (2010) book, *Cosmologies of Credit*, provides a wonderful ethnographic setting in which to think remittance houses in this way, particularly in their guise as a form of cultural capital that accrues status both to the migrant abroad and to in his or her relatives at home.

Chu (2010: 41–46) observes how in the village of Longyan, the site of her research in Fujian, a new generation of houses with reinforced-concrete frames and red-brick walls were built between 1978 and 1985, reflecting the new prosperity of the post-Mao Reform Era. But between the mid-1980s and the mid-1990s, these houses came to be surrounded by larger houses with ceramic-tiled exteriors built by those in the village receiving remittances from relatives in America. The formerly proud owners of the red-brick houses, which in their time were 'shining symbols of new prosperity,' now found themselves dwelling in structures that, outshone by the tiled houses around them, had morphed into 'the ramshackle signs of low living among newly imaginative structures of modern and cosmopolitan dwelling' (Chu 2010: 45).

Now seen as 'hopelessly crammed, dilapidated, and backward' (Chu 2010: 46), the newly passé red-brick houses of Longyan may seem but passive victims of changing human fashion. But are they mere objects of embarrassment for human subjects or have they assumed a new mode of agency in relation to those subjects? Where once, a mere decade previously, they caused their owners to swell with pride, now they cause them to shrink with shame. I use these common English descriptors of shame's affects – 'swell' and 'shrink' – because they capture the corporeality of affect. The implications of this affective relationality for the turnover of built fabric in Longyan suggest we may need to think of the temporality of migration heritage not in terms of migrant generations (e.g., the first-generation, second-generation interval) and even less in terms of the eras commonplace in heritage parlance (e.g., early 20th century or mid-20th century) but in terms of generations of built fabric and the temporality of waves of building fashion washing through diasporic space.

The causal sequence wherein the red-brick house acquires its capacity to embarrass is initiated, one might guess, in village society's tendency to assign social status partly according to the houses people occupy. The houses' agency thus derives from a particular social situation, but this in no way lessens the capacity of the red-brick houses of Longyan to cause their owners to cringe with embarrassment. These are real embodied affects triggered by real physical things.

For Chu (2010: 35), locality is 'a structure of feeling.' The process of migration stretches this structure such that houses in emigrant villages become actors imbricated in causal sequences of transnational scope. Village members overseas have laboured for the new houses and the social status they confer, and it is only by means of this labour that they and their relatives at home can escape the embarrassing, status-diminishing effects of the superseded 'old' houses, houses that in effect demand to be renovated, rebuilt or replaced. It is misleading to think of them as mere 'products' of the phenomenon of migration, a point that is also at the heart of Iván Sandoval-Cervantes' (2017) ethnographic study of remittance houses in Zegache village in Oaxaca, Mexico. While the houses may nourish a 'myth of return' (Miller 2008: 407) on the part of the emigrant, for those left behind they may be sites of 'active waiting' (Sandoval-Cervantes 2017: 210). Drawing on Berlant's concept of 'cruel optimism', Sandoval-Cervantes describes how such houses, especially those in an unfinished state, promise the return of those abroad who initiated them.

For relatives at home, including mothers of migrant sons, caring for the house built by the absent one is an aspect of active waiting and longing in which they are exposed to and respond to the affective intensities of the house (Sandoval-Cervantes 2017: 212). The absentee's presence is materialised in the house's fabric.

> The daily lives of the families of transnational migrants are constantly informed by actions and emotions that emerge from unfinished houses,

active awaiting, and the hopeful aspirations of the ever-present possibility of return migration and family reunification, as migrants build houses that seem to indicate their desire to return.

(Sandoval-Cervantes 2017: 215–216)

At least some of the early 20th-century remittance houses of south China that have been the subject of my own research are likely, in a similar way, to be embodiments of active waiting, but the turmoil and catastrophe of the mid-20th century in China have made it virtually impossible to reconstruct this aspect of their meaning. From a heritage studies perspective, what is important about the work of Chu and Sandoval-Cervantes is that it at least alerts us to the range of possible meanings that such buildings (many of them now passing into the realm of public heritage) have had for people living with them in the past and how these buildings spoke to them.

In proposing the migration heritage corridor as a useful concept in heritage practice, I do so on the understanding that we think of it as – in addition to its other characteristics – a structure of feeling. The relevance of feeling and affective relationality is not unappreciated in the heritage studies field as a whole (e.g., Byrne 2013; Crouch 2015; Tolia-Kelly, Waterton and Watson 2017) but these insights have so far failed to penetrate migration heritage as a field of study, where they might call into question the very idea of the bordered, nation-state container approach to the conservation and interpretation of that heritage.

Colonialism and social status: channelling the neoclassical in China

During the 1920s and 1930s, many of Zhongshan County's remittance houses were distinctive for their Western-style neoclassical façades, featuring porticoes and balconies supported by Greek columns. The architecture of these houses is discussed in detail in Chapter 3. Here attention is on the question of what architectural neoclassicism meant to those who built the houses; in particular, to those who emigrated to Australia and built the houses on return visits, built them 'remotely' via funds and instructions sent from Australia or built them upon becoming permanent returnees.

Zhongshan emigrants would have had plenty of opportunity to observe and frequent neoclassical buildings in Australia and yet there is no evidence that the neoclassical remittance houses of Zhongshan were directly inspired by those buildings rather than by examples of neoclassical architecture closer to Zhongshan itself. In Macao, Hong Kong and in the treaty ports of China, such as Shanghai and Xiamen, during the period spanning the late 19th and the early 20th century, Western architects had created neoclassic buildings, including houses, that provided 'architectural familiarity' for Western nationals resident there (Rowe and Kuan 2002: 30) and that symbolised the West's dominance in colonial or crypto-colonial space. The situation was comparable to British India where, according to Thomas Metcalf (1989), neoclassical architecture was deployed to express the spirit of empire and the relations of power that went with imperial subjugation.

Arguing that neoclassical architecture in China was not so much a direct import from the West as representative of an architecture of the larger colonial zone, Peter Rowe and Seng Kuan note that the 1908 railway station in Shanghai had 'close stylistic parallels' not just with its 'counterpart' in Bombay but also with Victorian public buildings in Melbourne and Hong Kong (Rowe and Kuan 2002: 33). By extension, it seems likely the migrant builders of neoclassical-style houses in Zhongshan were drawing inspiration not from Australia as a country and, from 1901, a nation, but from a colonial architectural milieu in which Australia participated. The relation of the houses to Australian architecture was likely one of simultaneity rather than of a unilinear flow of influence. The neoclassical architectural milieu of the British empire was a hybrid of metropolitan style and local influences, major among the latter being that of climate. These considerations caution against thinking of the China–Australia migration heritage corridor (of which the Zhongshan heritage corridor forms a strand) in a narrowly delineated manner. The Zhongshan–Australia corridor was certainly not insulated from colonial Southeast Asia, Britain's larger empire, or from the global Chinese diaspora, but it retains sufficient coherence to be useful as a concept.

British architecture in Hong Kong was a significant influence on the builders of Zhongshan remittance houses but their engagement with it took the form of a complex cultural exchange. People from Zhongshan traded with and worked in Hong Kong since the Crown Colony's inception in 1841. Many of them became important players in its economy and their mostly poorer relatives were among those who migrated to Australia. Almost all Zhongshan emigrants departed from Hong Kong port and when making return visits to China or returning to settle, they disembarked there en route to their home villages in Zhongshan. Many permanent returnees opted to settle in Hong Kong while maintaining close contact with their home villages. Hong Kong was indeed a key node or 'knot' (Ingold 2011) on migrant lifelines transecting the Zhongshan–Australia corridor. Although up until the late 20th century, most migrants to Australia originated in the villages rather than the cities of their origin countries, those villages have typically been entwined via histories of internal migration with the urban culture of their home country. All this set the scene for the emergence of a neoclassical migrant architecture in Zhongshan that was entwined with the changed social position of migrants and their village-based relatives, an architecture that can be seen to have been indirectly responsive to racial segregation in Hong Kong.

Under the British, Hong Kong was a racially segregated society, a situation illustrated by the law that between 1902 and 1946 prevented Chinese from living on Victoria Peak, a British residential enclave where colonial privilege was expressed in the neoclassical style of many of its houses (Carroll 2007: 74; Lai 2010). The colonial administration saw Chinese houses and European houses as 'mutually exclusive building types' belonging to clearly distinguished residential districts (Lai 2010: 53–55). In the pre-war era, the 'Chinese house' (*tong lau*) took the form of a three- or four-storey row house that was long and narrow in plan, typically with a shop on the ground floor and accommodation on the upper floors, often in the form of tenements occupied by recent migrants from the Chinese mainland (Chu 2012: 255). Cecelia Chu (2012) describes these buildings as a hybrid of the 'traditional townhouses of South China' and a modern commercial style designed by their builders (mostly Chinese) to take advantage of the opportunities of Hong Kong's fast-expanding economy while at the same time complying with the colony's discriminatory zoning regulations. The colonial zoning laws in Hong Kong determined that only the 'European' type house, typically a detached dwelling surrounded by gardens, could be built in Hong Kong Island's 'hill district' which included The Peak, and while Chinese were permitted to buy properties there, which many did, they could only live in them with the consent of the government, which up until 1946 was never granted (Lai 2010: 58).

Key to explaining the neoclassical style of migrant-built houses in Zhongshan is the fact that while wealthy Chinese residents in Hong Kong, including returned migrants, could not live in areas reserved for white colonists there was nothing to stop them from appropriating the 'architecture of privilege' found in those zones for the houses they built for themselves in areas outside them. For example, James Choy Hing (1869–1957), a returned migrant from Australia and co-founder of the Sincere department store chain, in 1915 built himself a grand neoclassical mansion at No. 2 Park Street in the Mid-Levels on Hong Kong Island that easily rivalled in neoclassical grandeur the houses of the British on The Peak (Bellis 2015). Beyond symbolising white privilege, within local Chinese society neoclassical style came to symbolise wealth and success. While in the emigrant villages of Zhongshan County, neoclassical style stood for wealth and success gained through migration, it also carried the cachet of the new and the modern, qualities whose attraction to Chinese migrants of the time in Australia is discussed in detail in Chapter 5.

But the agency shown by Chinese in Hong Kong and migrant builders in Zhongshan in appropriating the neoclassical style should not be allowed to distract from the fact that that style was imbued with the power relations of colonialism. It would be naïve to think the Chinese adoption of the neoclassical was the outcome of a neutral choice, any more than it was a matter of neutral choice that Chinese migrants in Sydney adapted themselves to existing Anglo-Australian architecture rather than constructing buildings more amenable to their lifestyle. In Hong Kong, wealthy Chinese were almost obliged to live in neoclassical houses if they wanted to elevate their social status; in Sydney, anti-Chinese sentiment among Anglo-Australians meant Chinese migrants, to avoid standing out, were more inclined to blend themselves into local architecture than produce an architecture of their own. Neither in Hong Kong nor in Sydney was the built environment a level playing field for those Chinese who were striving to better themselves.

Sara Ahmed (2007), drawing on the work of Edmund Husserl and Franz Fanon, lays out an argument for the way non-white bodies become oriented to a world that colonialism has made white. 'Colonialism makes the world "white", which is of course a world "ready" for certain kinds of bodies, as a world that puts certain objects within their reach' (Ahmed 2007: 154). The way whiteness works, in Ahmed's account, is by creating an environment – for present purposes this can be taken to include the *built* environment – that is amenable to and comfortably 'reachable' by white people but not to non-white people without an effort. It is a world oriented to the needs and habits of whites but requires a *re*-orientation on the part of non-whites if they want to succeed in it. In Ahmed's (2007: 158) words, 'White bodies are comfortable *as they inhabit spaces that extend their shape*. The bodies and spaces point towards each other' (italics in the original). Ahmed's (2007) 'phenomenology of whiteness' is useful in thinking the specifics of how neoclassical architectural style was adopted and adapted by those Chinese in Hong Kong who wanted to succeed in colonial space and society. Writing of the houses built by wealthy Chinese in British colonial Malaya, David Kohl suggests that Chinese migrants there may not have appreciated the architectural association of these houses with ancient Greek and Roman culture, but they did understand the weighty connotations of social status that this style carried (Kohl 2018).[5]

But to explain how it came to be adopted in the emigrant villages of Zhongshan County, outside the colonial space of Hong Kong, requires further explanation. I suggest it was the outcome of a process in which neoclassical architecture had become, in Lévi-Strauss's terms, a 'floating signifier' (Mehlman 1972), meaning in this case that while in the colonial setting it signified race status and the subversion of that by Chinese subalterns, by the time it reached Zhongshan's emigrant villages it had been emptied, or largely emptied, of this specificity and simply signified social status accrued through migration. Whereas in Hong Kong, the neoclassicism of the Chinese entrepreneur's house made a direct allusion to white status and power, in Zhongshan this allusion was weak or non-existent. This appears also to have been true of houses built by migrants in their home villages in Fujian during the 1930s (Chen 1940: 109–111). Through their donations to the building or repair of ancestral halls, schools and other community infrastructure, migrant families by the early 1900s were assuming something of the role and status of the old gentry class of China (Cheng 2020; Williams 2018: 88–89). This work of sponsorship elevated their social status. But the house, and particularly its façade, could function in the village setting as a more direct material statement of the status, or aspirant status, of an individual or family.

As argued at the beginning of this chapter, the heritage landscape of Chinese migration is constituted in assemblages of human and nonhuman agents that are transnational in scope. Part of the complex meaning of neoclassical style in Western culture was carried into remittance houses in Zhongshan via the agency of their builders and the agency invested in architectural elements such as Greek-style pillars and porticoes as floating signifiers of race-related social status. The houses, which at face value may seem to be no more than heritage objects representing specific migrant trajectories, must also be credited as embodiments of broader transnational flows and forces, including those of colonialism. The chapter that follows, with its detailed appraisal of the materiality of Zhongshan remittance houses, takes the reader closer to them and to their situatedness in the context of migrancy.

Notes

1 Boccagni and Murcia (2021: 3) make a very similar point, describing remittance houses in Ecuador as being 'expected to social [sic] compensate migrants' physical absence and to publicly display their commitment to return in the future.'
2 Here I draw on Lynn Meskell's (2004) book, *Object Worlds in Ancient Egypt*.
3 Migration Data Portal, 2021. https://migrationdataportal.org/themes/remittances.
4 The Hong Kong–China border was drawn when in 1898, following the Second Opium War, when Britain negotiated the lease of the New Territories.
5 For an account of the link between social status and new houses in Fujian in the 1930s, see Chen (1940).

References

Ahmed, Sara. 2006. *Queer Phenomenology: Orientations, Objects, Others*. Durham, NC: Duke University Press.
Ahmed, Sara. 2007. 'A phenomenology of whiteness,' *Feminist Theory* 8(2): 149–168, https://doi.org/10.1093/acprof:oso/9780199734771.001.0001.

Ahmed, Sara. 2010. 'Happy objects,' in Melissa Gregg and Gregory J. Seigworth (eds.), *The Affect Reader*, pp. 29–51. Durham, NC: Duke University Press.

Ang, Ien. 2011. 'Unsettling the national: Heritage and diaspora,' in Helmut Anheier and Yudhishthir Raj Isar (eds.), *Heritage, Memory and Identity*, pp. 82–94. London: Sage.

Bellis, David. 2015. 'Breezy point, 2 park road,' *Gwulo: Old Hong Kong*, blog accessed July 2019, https://gwulo.com/node/23308#14/22.2839/114.1826/Map_by_ESRI-Markers/100

Bennett, Jane. 2010. *Vibrant Matter: A Political Ecology of Things*. Durham, NC: Duke University Press.

Boccagni, Paolo and Luis Eduardo Pérez Murcia. 2021. 'Fixed places, shifting distances: Remittance houses and migrants' negotiation of home in Ecuador,' *Migration Studies* 9(1): 47–64, https://doi.org/ 10.1093/migration/mnaa017.

Bryant, Levy. 2011. *The Democracy of Objects*. Ann Arbor, MI: Open Humanities Press, http://dx.doi.org/10.3998/ohp.9750134.0001.001.

Byrne, Denis. 2013. 'Love and loss in the 1960s,' *International Journal of Heritage Studies* 19(6): 596–609, https://doi.org/10.1080/13527258.2012.686446.

Byrne, Denis. 2016. 'Heritage corridors: Transnational flows and the built environment of migration,' *Journal of Ethnic and Migration Studies* 42(14): 2351–2369, https://doi.org/10.1080/1369183X.2016.1205805.

Byrne, Denis and Heather Goodall. 2013. 'Placemaking and transnationalism: Recent migrants and a national park in Sydney, Australia,' *Parks: The International Journal of Protected Areas and Conservation* 19(1): 63–72, https://doi.org/10.2305/IUCN.CH.2013.PARKS-19-1.DB.en.

Carroll, John M. 2007. *A Concise History of Hong Kong*. Lanham, MD: Rowman and Littlefield.

Chen, Ta. 1940. *Emigrant Communities in South China: A Study of Overseas Migration and Its Influence on Standards of Living and Social Change*. New York: Institute for Pacific Relations.

Cheng, Christopher. 2020. 'Beacons of modern learning: Diaspora-funded schools in the China-Australia corridor,' *Asian and Pacific Migration Journal* 29(2): 139–162, https://doi.org/10.1177/0117196820930309.

Chu, Cecilia. 2012. 'Between typologies and representation: The *Tong Lau* and the discourse of the "Chinese house" in colonial Hong Kong,' in Mrinalini Rajagopalan and Madhuri Desai (eds.), *Colonial Frames, Nationalist Histories: Imperial Legacies, Architecture, and Modernity*, pp. 253–283. Farnham, UK: Ashgate.

Chu, Julie Y. 2010. *Cosmologies of Credit: Transnational Mobility and the Politics of Destination in China*. Durham, NC: Duke University Press.

Cohen, Jeffrey H. 2001. 'Transnational migration in rural Oaxaca, Mexico: Dependency, development, and the household,' *American Anthropologist* 103(4): 954–967, https://doi.org/10.1525/aa.2001.103.4.954.

Connerton, Paul. 1989. *How Societies Remember*. Cambridge: Cambridge University Press.

Coole, Diana. 2010. 'The inertia of matter and the generativity of flesh,' in D. Coole and S. Frost (eds.), *New Materialisms: Ontology, Agency, and Politics*, pp. 92–115. Durham, NC: Duke University Press.

Crouch, David. 2015. 'Affect, heritage, feeling,' in Emma Waterton and Steve Watson (eds.), *The Palgrave Handbook of Contemporary Heritage Research*, pp. 177–190. Houndmills, UK: Palgrave Macmillan.

Datta, Ayona. 2008. 'Building differences: Material geographies of home(s) among Polish builders in London,' *Transactions of the Institute of British Geographers* 33: 518–531, https://doi.org/10.1111/j.1475-5661.2008.00320.x.

DeLanda, Manuel. 2016. *Assemblage Theory*. Edinburgh: Edinburgh University Press.

Enfield, Nick J. 2017. 'Distribution of agency,' in N. J. Enfield and Paul Kockelman (eds.). *Distributed Agency*, pp. 9–14. Oxford: Oxford University Press.

Forty, Adrian. 2012. *Concrete and Culture: A Material History*. London: Reaktion.

Gell, Alfred. 1998. *Art and Agency: An Anthropological Theory*. Oxford: Oxford University Press.

Goodall, Heather, Stephen Wearing, Denis Byrne and Allison Cadzow. 2009. 'Fishing the Georges River: Cultural diversity and urban environments,' in Amanda Wise and Selvaraj Velayutham (eds.), *Everyday Multiculturalism*, pp. 177–196. Houndmills, UK: Palgrave Macmillan.

Hsu, Madeline Y. 2000. *Dreaming of Gold, Dreaming of Home: Transnationalism and Migration Between the United States and South China 1882–1943*. Stanford: Stanford University Press.

Ingold, Tim. 2008. 'Bindings against boundaries: Entanglements of life in an open world,' *Environment and Planning A* 40: 1796–1810, https://doi.org/10.1068/a40156.

Ingold, Tim. 2011. *Being Alive: Essays on Movement, Knowledge and Description*. Abingdon, UK: Routledge.

Johnson, G. E. and Yuen-fong Woon. 1997. 'The response to rural reform in an overseas Chinese area: Examples from two localities in the western Pearl River Delta region, South China,' *Modern Asian Studies* 31(1): 31–59.

Kohl, David G. 2018. *Offshore Chinese Architecture: Insights on Five Centuries of Overseas Chinese Building Practices*. Portland, OR: One Spirit.

Kuhn, Philip. 2008. *Chinese Among Others: Emigration in Modern Times*. Lanham, MD: Rowman and Littlefield.

Lai, Lawrence W. C. 2010. 'Discriminatory zoning in colonial Hong Kong: A review of the post-war literature and some further evidence for an economic theory of discrimination,' *Property Management* 29(1): 50–86, https://doi.org/10.1108/02637471111102932.

Latour, Bruno. 1993. *We Have Never Been Modern*. Cambridge, MA: Harvard University Press.

Levitt, Peggy and Nina Glick Schiller. 2004. 'Conceptualizing simultaneity: A transnational social field perspective on society,' *International Migration Review* 38(3): 1002–1039, https://doi.org/1002-1039.10.1111/j.1747–7379.2004.tb00227.x.

Lopez, Sarah. 2010. 'The remittance house: Architecture of migration in rural Mexico,' *Built Landscapes* 17(2): 33–52.

Lopez, Sarah. 2015. *The Remittance Landscape: Spaces of Migration in Rural Mexico and Urban USA*. Chicago: University of Chicago Press.

Lozanovska, Mirjana. 2019. *Migrant Housing: Architecture, Dwelling, Migration.* London: Routledge.

McKeown, Adam. 2001. *Chinese Migrant Networks and Cultural Change: Peru, Chicago, Hawaii, 1900–1936.* Chicago: University of Chicago Press.

Mehlman, Jeffrey. 1972. 'The "floating signifier": From Lévi-Strauss to Lacan,' *Yale French Studies* 48: 10–37.

Meskell, Lynn. 2004. *Object Worlds in Ancient Egypt: Material Biographies Past and Present.* Oxford: Berg.

Metcalf, Thomas. 1989. *An Imperial Vision: Indian Architecture and Britain's Raj.* Berkeley: University of California Press.

Miller, Daniel. 2008. 'Migration, material culture and tragedy: Four moments in Caribbean migration,' *Mobilities* 3(3): 397–413, https://doi.org/10.1080/174501 00802376712.

Rowe, Peter G. and Seng Kuan. 2002. *Architectural Encounters with Essence and Form in Modern China.* Cambridge, MA: MIT Press.

Sandell, David P. 2010. 'Where mourning takes them: Migrants, borders, and an alternative reality,' *Ethos* 38(2): 179–204, https://doi.org/10.1111/j.1548-1352. 2010.01135.x.

Sandoval-Cervantes, Iván. 2017. 'Uncertain futures: The unfinished houses of undocumented migrants in Oaxaca, Mexico,' *American Anthropologist* 119(2): 209–222, https://doi.org/10.1111/aman.12864.

Seigworth, Gregory J. and Melissa Gregg. 2010. 'An inventory of shimmers,' in Melissa Gregg and Gregory J. Seigworth (eds.), *The Affect Theory Reader,* pp. 1–25. Durham, NC: Duke University Press.

Strathern, Marilyn. 1988. *The Gender of the Gift: Problems with Women and Problems with Society in Melanesia.* Berkeley: University of California Press.

Taylor, Steve. 2015. '"Home is never fully achieved . . . even when we are in it": Migration, belonging and social exclusion within Punjabi transnational mobility,' *Mobilities* 10: 193–210, https://doi.org/10.1080/17450101.2013.848606.

Tolia-Kelly, Divya, Emma Waterton and Steve Watson (eds.). 2017. *Heritage, Affect and Emotion: Policies, Practices and Infrastructures.* London: Routledge.

Tsuda, Takeyuki. 2012. 'Whatever happened to simultaneity? Transnational migration theory and dual engagement in sending and receiving countries,' *Journal of Ethnic and Migration Studies* 38(4): 631–649, https://doi.org/10.1080/13691 83X.2012.659126.

Vertovec, Stephen. 2004. 'Migrant transnationalism and modes of transformation,' *International Migration Review* 38(4): 970–1001, https://doi.org/10.1111/j.1747-7379.2004.tb00226.x.

Ward, Peter, W. 2013. 'Stature, migration and human welfare in South China, 1850–1930,' *Economics and Human Biology* 11: 488–501, https://doi.org/10.1016/j.ehb.2012.10.003.

Watson, James L. 1975. *Emigration and the Chinese Lineage: The Mans in Hong Kong and London.* Berkeley: University of California Press.

Watson, James L. 2004. 'Presidential address: Virtual kinship, real estate, and diaspora formation – the Man lineage revisited,' *Journal of Asian Studies* 63(4): 893–910.

Williams, Michael. 2003. 'In the Tang Mountains we have a big house,' *East Asian History* 25/26: 85–112.

Williams, Michael. 2018. *Returning Home with Glory: Chinese Villagers Around the Pacific, 1849 to 1949*. Hong Kong: Hong Kong University Press.

Witmore, Christopher. 2014. 'Archaeology and the new materialisms,' *Journal of Contemporary Archaeology* 1(2): 203–246, https://doi.org/10.1558/jca.v1i2.16661.

Woon, Yuen-fong. 1984. *Social Organization in South China, 1911–1949: The Case of the Kuan Lineage of K'ai-p'ing County*. Ann Arbor, MI: Center for Chinese Studies, University of Michigan.

3 Dream houses in Zhongshan

This chapter describes the houses constructed in the villages of Zhongshan County by those who had migrated from there to Australia. As I will show, the houses have their architectural origins in the vernacular houses of southern China but by the end of the 19th century they began to incorporate self-consciously modern design elements. Indeed, the houses reflect the aspirational modernity that so inflected the lives of those who left Zhongshan for overseas destinations. The very act of leaving represented a desire for a better life, which at this time in history was virtually synonymous with a modern life.

The houses were built in the last decades of the Qing Dynasty (1644–1911) and during the Republican era (1912–1949), though a few were constructed after the Japanese occupied the Pearl River Delta in 1938. They often stood in the same village streets as houses built by those who had migrated to Hawaii, California, Cuba or Canada. Migrant destination locales maintain a presence in the villages partly in the habit villagers have of referring to particular houses using the terms 'Australian house', 'Hawaiian house' and so on. Throughout the book, I refer to the houses as 'remittance houses', bearing in mind, however, that some were built by those returning to their village on a visit or by returned migrants using money repatriated rather than remitted from Australia or, in a few cases, with money earned after their return. The scale of remittance building in southern China in the early 20th century was truly impressive, one commentator observing that in the city of Xiamen in Fujian Province more than 5,300 new homes were built in the four years from 1928, over 90 percent of them with overseas Chinese capital (Cook 2008: 140).

Remittance houses in their modern and transnational aspects

To reiterate a point made in the previous chapter, like migrant bodies, the material objects and places of migration might be said to simultaneously

DOI: 10.4324/9781003088714-4

'face' both the destination and origin locale (Ahmed 2006). The remittance houses in the emigrant villages of Zhongshan are oriented simultaneously towards the village and towards those buildings and places in San Francisco or Sydney where Chinese migrants dreamt of them, planned them and laboured to earn money to construct them. As well as providing accommodation for family members who have stayed behind in the villages, remittance houses act as placeholders for absent migrants themselves, lending them a 'proxy presence' there (Dalakoglou 2010). This *presencing* aspect of the remittance house goes beyond what in heritage practice is known as the associative value of a heritage place, which refers to the connections a certain place has to particular people or events in the past (e.g., Fredheim and Khalaf 2016: 473). The migrant builder is not, however, merely associated or connected with the remittance house, the house is a material instantiation or embodiment of the migrant.

The temporality most often employed in the heritage perspective is one of anteriority, a view backwards from the present that surveys the material past and consolidates it as legacy. However, being deeply informed by 'the politics of loss,' this optic is also inevitably implicated, via the anticipation of loss, in a futuring (future making) perspective (DeSilvey and Harrison 2020). In the case of the early mid-20th-century remittance houses of Zhongshan County, both heritage officials and migrant descendants concerned about the fate of the houses can be assumed to be caught up in this kind of time compression, a mutually enfolded past–present–future. It is interesting in this context to consider the position of those who built the houses, and in this respect Sandoval-Cervantes' (2017) ethnography of houses built by migrants in their home villages in Oaxaca, referred to in the previous chapter, offers seminal ideas. He describes the houses, many of which linger for years in an unfinished state, as an attempt to give spatial-material form to migrants' hopes for the future. For Sandoval-Cervantes, the houses are an expression of patience, which resonates with Appadurai's description of the migrant experience as one of waiting for a better future.[1] As far as the China–Australia migration corridor is concerned, in the late 1800s and early 1900s a better future meant a modern future.

We should keep this in mind as we come to regard old remittance houses as heritage items. As expressions of future-making, they have a particular temporality. They also have a particular transnational spatiality deriving from the fact that the planning, waiting and hoping that they embody was for the most part distributed and shared across the span of migration corridors. But migration is experienced differently by different people. We know, for example, that by no means all Chinese immigrants in Australia built houses in their ancestral villages, whether that was because they could not afford the expense or because they simply had no desire to build them.

Zhongshan's remittance houses of the pre-1940s era, in their various types, form a remarkably intact array, partly courtesy of the hiatus in house-building activity during the Mao era, as discussed at the end of the chapter. This contrasts with the situations in some other migrant-sending countries. In Greece, for example, houses built in their home villages by those who had departed to places abroad in the period 1890 to 1924 were mostly destroyed in World War II and the Greek Civil War that followed (Kourelis 2020: 88, 99).

Zhongshan remittance houses 1890s–1940s: a typology

In the early years of Chinese migration to Australia, remittances were often sent home to relatives in the form of gold entrusted to friends and clansmen, but by the late 1800s it was common for payments to be made to Chinese shop owners in Australia who consolidated small payments into drafts on Hong Kong banks. Some of these banks had branches in Shekki, Zhongshan's county town (Williams 2018: 100–103). The first priority of emigrants was the support of relatives left behind; the proportion of remittances devoted to house-building in Zhongshan was in the order of 20 percent (Williams 2018: 78). Remittances were also used for buying agricultural land, either for farming or as the site for a new house. A survey of land holdings carried out around 1950 in the emigrant areas of Guangdong, including Zhongshan County, found that overseas families owned between 0.5 and 3.2 acres of land compared to only 0.2 to 0.3 acres among non-migrant families (Peterson 2012: 44).

The houses described in what follows were identified in the field using information provided by the descendants of Zhongshan emigrants in Australia and with the aid of village officials, elderly residents of the villages and the staff of the Zhongshan office of the Bureau of Overseas Chinese Affairs. I have ordered the houses into four types, based on their physical, architectural attributes. The typology represents an overlapping temporal sequence: Type 1 first appearing in the late 1800s, followed by Type 2 in the 1910s, Type 3 in the 1920s and Type 4 in the 1930s. With the exception of the Type 1 house, which seems not to have been built after about 1900, the house types were being produced simultaneously up till the 1940s, the difference between them reflecting the different means and ambitions of their creators.

Prior to setting off for overseas destinations, Zhongshan emigrants had overwhelmingly been farmers, cultivating their own few fields or renting fields from landlords. They lived in small houses that were mostly on rectangular plots of land measuring about four metres wide by 15 metres deep. These differed from vernacular houses in some other parts of China in their lack of an internal courtyard.[2] The houses were separated by narrow spaces or were conjoined to form rows of houses lining the typically narrow lanes of the village. The typical village was a compact cluster of houses with one or two temples and ancestral halls set among them, surrounded by rice fields. The single-storey vernacular houses, which represented the baseline from which remittance houses departed, had walls of sun-dried mud bricks and gabled roofs covered with straw thatch or ceramic tiles.[3] The walls of the houses of some of the better off peasant farmers were made of kiln-fired red brick or a combination of red brick for the lower wall and mud brick for the higher portion. The façade had a central doorway but no windows, and the ridge of the gable roof paralleled the façade. In some of the poorer, non-emigrant villages of the Pearl River Delta, this type of house was still standard until the 1970s (Chan, Madsen and Unger 2009: 256). Today, very few survive in Zhongshan, even as ruins.

Type 1: the stretched traditional house

By the 1890s, a recognisably distinct remittance house had emerged that was a larger version of the vernacular house described earlier, though built using a more durable and expensive type of brick, grey in colour, that had been favoured by the elite in Zhongshan since Ming times. Built on the same plots of land as the older houses they replaced, the new houses could only be larger by virtue of being higher. While some of the older houses had a loft, reached by a ladder and extending over the back half of the front room, in the Type 1 house this loft grows to become a mezzanine in a front room that has approximately doubled in height. A semi-transparent wooden screen wall separates the mezzanine from the front room. Back from the mezzanine in some of the houses are upper storey bedrooms under a second gable. Effectively this is a two-storey house fitted into the template of the single-storey traditional house, but its two-storey interior is disguised from the street by a façade identical to that of the former except in being higher (Figure 3.1). The same style of doorway is present, sometimes with a 'transom light' window above it, but is stretched higher in accord with the heightened façade.

This type of house, staying within the conventions of the vernacular while stretching the template, might be said to be simultaneously an expression of sameness and an assertion of difference. It represents the flow of new money into the emigrant village, but this money does not translate as architectural ostentation. From a heritage, and indeed an archaeological perspective, the importance of this house type lies in it being one of a series of types that together tell a story of increasing wealth flowing across the migration corridor into Zhongshan.

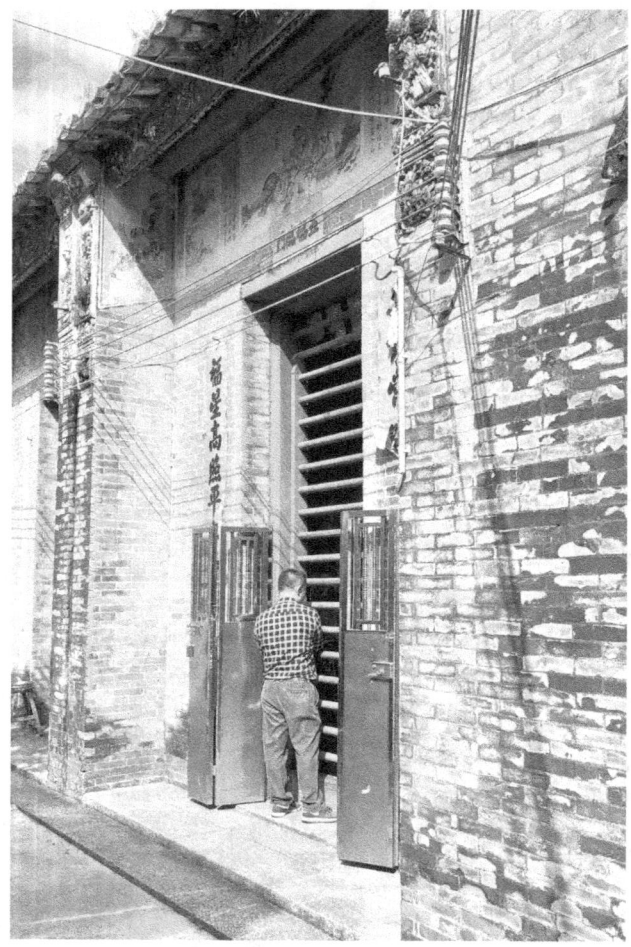

Figure 3.1 Type 1 house, built in Caobian village by a migrant based in Queensland.

Type 2: the large two-storey house

This is a fully realised two-storey house which, while stylistically continuous with Type 1, is significantly larger and internally more elaborate. Emerging in the 1910s, almost all these houses are free-standing, the larger of them being located on what would then have been the edge of their villages where fields had been purchased for their construction (Figure 3.2).

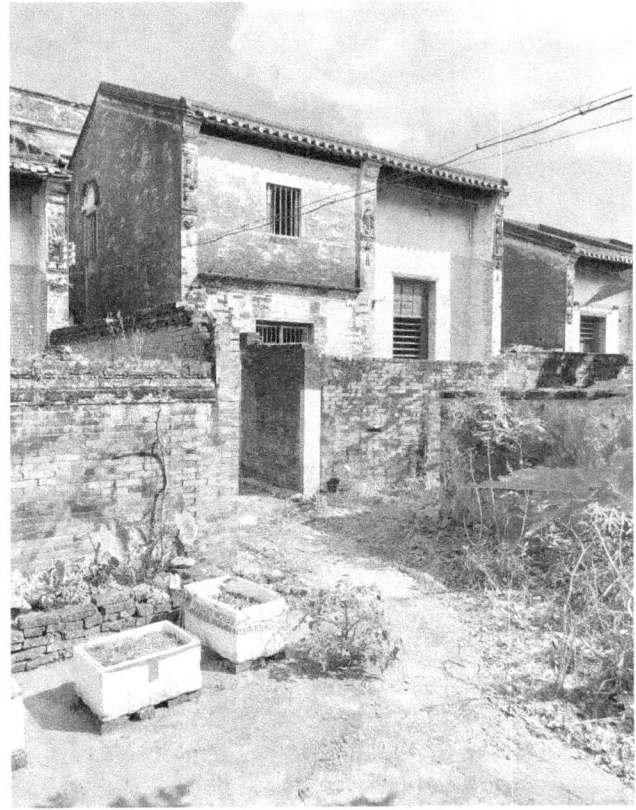

Figure 3.2 Type 2 house, built by a migrant to Australia, Caobian village.

Many adopt a duplex form, built to accommodate the families of brothers in accord with an embedded social ideal that brothers should remain close residentially, something that in northern China would have been achieved by extending their father's single-storey courtyard house laterally. The façade typically features two high doors along with small windows on the upper level. As with the Type 1 house, the front room is an open space spanning the full height of the house, from the floor (which may be of wooden boards or ceramic tiles on concrete) to the exposed roof beams above.

In common with the Type 1 house, these houses have decorative friezes under the eaves, consisting of stucco relief mouldings and paintings of auspicious fruit, flowers and animals and auspicious non-figurative symbols. A range of landscape motifs commonly appear on the panels of the wooden screen walls of the interior. By the 1920s and 1930s, steamships and motor buses, emblems of mobility and modernity (the two were elided, see Chapter 5), sometimes feature in these landscapes (Figure 3.3). The screen walls often also have 'panels' of textured coloured glass, 'reverse painted' with symbols and landscape scenes, along with unpainted glass mirrors.[4] Glass mirrors were being imported by China by the 1880s and were mass-produced there during Republican times (Dikötter 2007: 185–186).

Some Type 2 houses incorporate watchtowers, or *diaolou*, rising two or more levels above the roof. They were used for refuge during attacks by bandits attracted to emigrant villages by their remittance-fuelled wealth. Such attacks became widespread in Zhongshan in the 1920s and 1930s (Williams 2018: 90–91). The towers are smaller and less elaborate than those of Kaiping County, 60 kilometres southwest of Zhongshan, an array of which was included on the World Heritage list in 2007.[5]

Modernity is represented in these houses partly in the form of light. Glazed windows were typically let into the walls on both floors. Flat glass (also known as 'plated') had been adopted by the elite in China from the mid-1900s and by Republican times had been taken up by the lower classes, with hundreds of new glass factories springing up in China to cater to the demand (Dikötter 2007: 156). The windows tended to be small, but they brought light into spaces where the only other source of illumination was the oil lamp. Equating light with modernity in China, Frank Dikötter (2007: 165) notes that increased illumination permitted such modern activities as reading (with the spread of modern schooling, literacy increased dramatically at this time) and the crafting of new style clothes using foot-pedal sewing machines that quickly became de rigueur items in remittance houses. The British had installed an electric lighting plant in Canton (Guangzhou) by 1901 (Tsin 2001: 25), and in Zhongshan lamps were superseded by electricity in some remittance houses by around the 1910s. Jan See Chin, who migrated to Queensland from Ho Tau village, Zhongshan, returned there in 1915 and in the 1920s drew on the wealth that he had accumulated from his Queensland sugar plantations to build an electric power plant for the village (Wong 2018: 144).

The architectural vernacular is strongly apparent in these houses and yet they also clearly materialise particular modern ideas and practices. The houses are hybrid entities that defy understanding in terms of the conventional traditional–modern dualism. The entwinement or 'confusion' of the traditional and the modern in them parallels that found in indigenous architecture in late colonial India (Hosagrahar 2005). Because of their overall size and height, they would have been standout structures in the emigrant

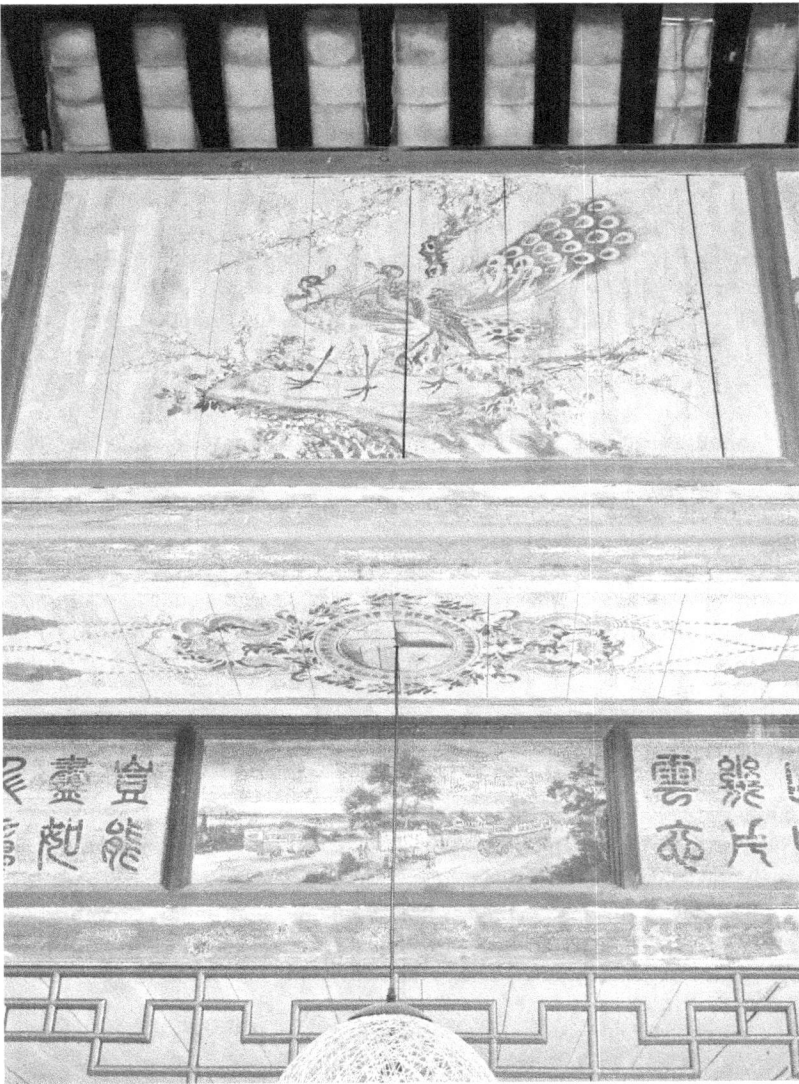

Figure 3.3 Paintings on wooden wall boards in a Type 2 house, Caobian village. Buses are depicted in the panel at bottom centre.

villages of the early 20th century, making a clear gesture to the relative affluence of those at the other end of the migration corridor whose wealth enabled their construction.

Type 3: the portico-balcony house

By the 1920s in Zhongshan County's emigrant villages, a larger version of the Type 2 house appeared, rendered dramatically distinctive by the grafting onto its front of a European neoclassical-style portico and first-floor balcony (Figure 3.4). Neoclassical influence, discussed more fully in Chapter 2, may have first filtered through to Zhongshan from the foreign enclave in Canton where it was in evidence from the 18th century (Farris 2007: 15). Closer to Zhongshan, in Hong Kong by the late 1800s neoclassical style was dominant in the architecture of public and commercial buildings as well as in many of the houses of the Chinese and Western elite.

The architectural ostentation of the neoclassical façades of the Type 3 houses allowed their owners to display the wealth that their offshore lives had brought them and to make implicit claims to an elevated status in the village. In reality, the building of them sometimes overextended the migrant's finances. As Adam McKeown (2001: 74) observes, most of the migrants failed to tell villagers at home how difficult their lives were abroad: 'Rather, they devoted much of their time at home to conspicuous consumption, providing entertainment and banquets for friends and villages, renovating their homes, showing off the sewing machines, radios and cameras they brought for their families.'

It was common for the interior walls and the ceilings of these houses to be painted with auspicious symbols and landscape scenes, similar to those in the more elaborate Type 2 houses, except here the landscapes tend to be painted in Western rather than traditional Chinese perspective (Figure 3.5). The traditional tiled gable roof of the Type 1 and 2 house is retained, except where the front gable has been replaced with a flat, reinforced concrete roof. While a few of the Type 2 houses have concrete floor plates, here they are prevalent and the entire portico-balcony element is of stucco-rendered reinforced concrete, including the neoclassical columns. In the larger houses, the entire structure is based on a reinforced concrete frame. Most of the internal walls are of brick and plaster though wooden screen walls are also used (Figure 3.5). The provision of masonry interior walls, according to Dikötter (2007: 160–161), reflects changing notions of the privacy of individuals within the family in Republican China and of the home as a 'repository of the individual.' But in contrast to the inward-looking traditional houses, the balconies of this type of house represent a semi-opening of the house to the outer world. Where they existed, the flat portions of the roof

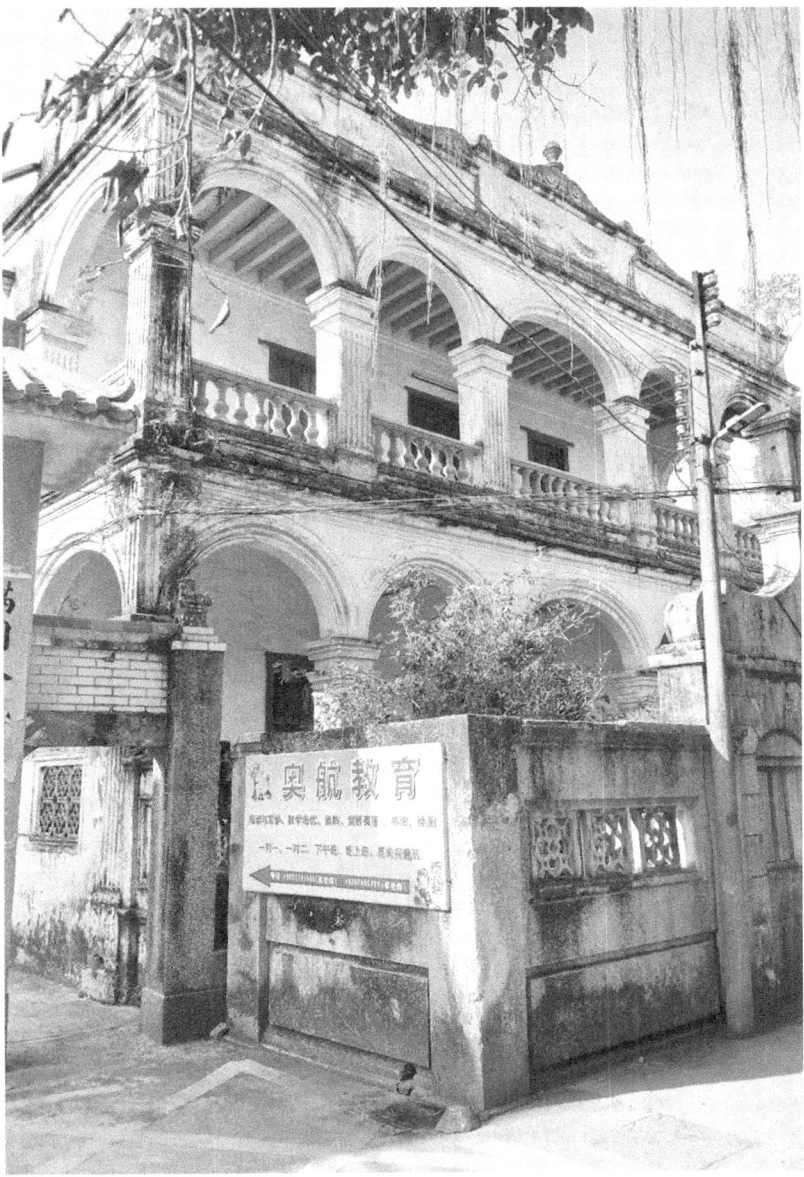

Figure 3.4 Type 3 portico-balcony house, built in Ho Tau village by Jan See Chin, a migrant who had returned from Queensland.

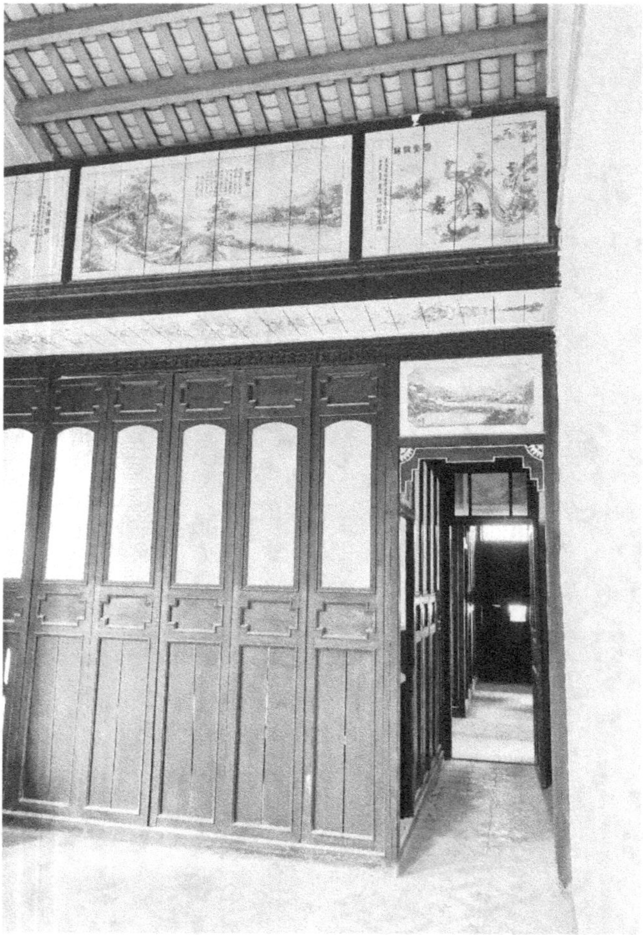

Figure 3.5 Upstairs room in a Type 3 house showing screen walls with textured glass.

were used recreationally and for sun-drying grain, vegetables and meat. Along with the windows in the upper floors, the flat roofs afforded the novelty of being able to observe village life from above. In more contemporary times, Xiaoyang Zhu (2014: 127) has referred to the flat roofs of post-1990s houses near Kunming, Yunnan, as 'sky patios' that represent the relocation upwards of the old-style internal courtyard.

In terms of the Western architectural canon, the grafting of a neoclassical façade onto a semi-vernacular gable-roofed house might seem to render the design incoherent, but as Hosagrahar (2005: 7) points out, the unsettling of architectural certainties has been an essential element of indigenous modernities in the Global South. The portico-balcony houses of Zhongshan, with their radically novel façades and the sheer stylistic variety of those façades, along with the inclusion of reinforced concrete and terrazzo elements, called for new construction skills that are likely to have been sourced from Hong Kong, where the construction labour force came mainly from neighbouring areas of the Pearl River Delta to which these skills are in turn likely to have filtered back (Chan-Yeung 2017: 73). In at least a few cases, architects were retained from Hong Kong to design the houses; otherwise, they were designed by their owners and by local builders.[6] The standardisation of building form and technology, which had been a hallmark of traditional Chinese architecture (Denison 2017: 94), was giving way in the new houses to a diversification in such things as the dimensions and arrangement of rooms and internal and external decoration. This bestowed a greater individualism on them than is seen in the Type 1 or Type 2 house. This accords with Dikötter's (2007: 187) observation that in China at this time, 'new materials and new ideas allowed enormous diversification of the architectural landscape in design, layout and substance.'

By the 1920s, a number of the migrant-built portico-balcony houses in Zhongshan were connected to the local electricity grid and to the piped water network, infrastructure which, so emblematic of modernity, was only possible to install in emigrant villages and in Shekki town because of the wealth flowing in from overseas Zhongshanese. It not only changed the pattern of domestic life but it also meant that the previously autonomous house became networked into and dependent upon an external infrastructural assemblage. The emigrant village itself had begun to function as a technological assemblage requiring new kinds of municipal governance (Tsin 2001).

Type 4: the mansion house

On a larger and grander scale than any of the other houses built in Zhongshan were two mansions constructed there by department store tycoons. Ma Ying Piu, one of the founders of the Sincere chain of department stores, in 1929 retained a Hong Kong architect to build a three-storey Palladian style house on the edge of Hengmei village. A few years later, the Kwok brothers, founders of the Wing On chain, built a three-storey Art Deco style mansion in their ancestral village, Zhuxiuyuan (Figure 3.6). Each of the Four Great Companies (Sincere, Wing On, Sun and Sun Sun) that ran department stores

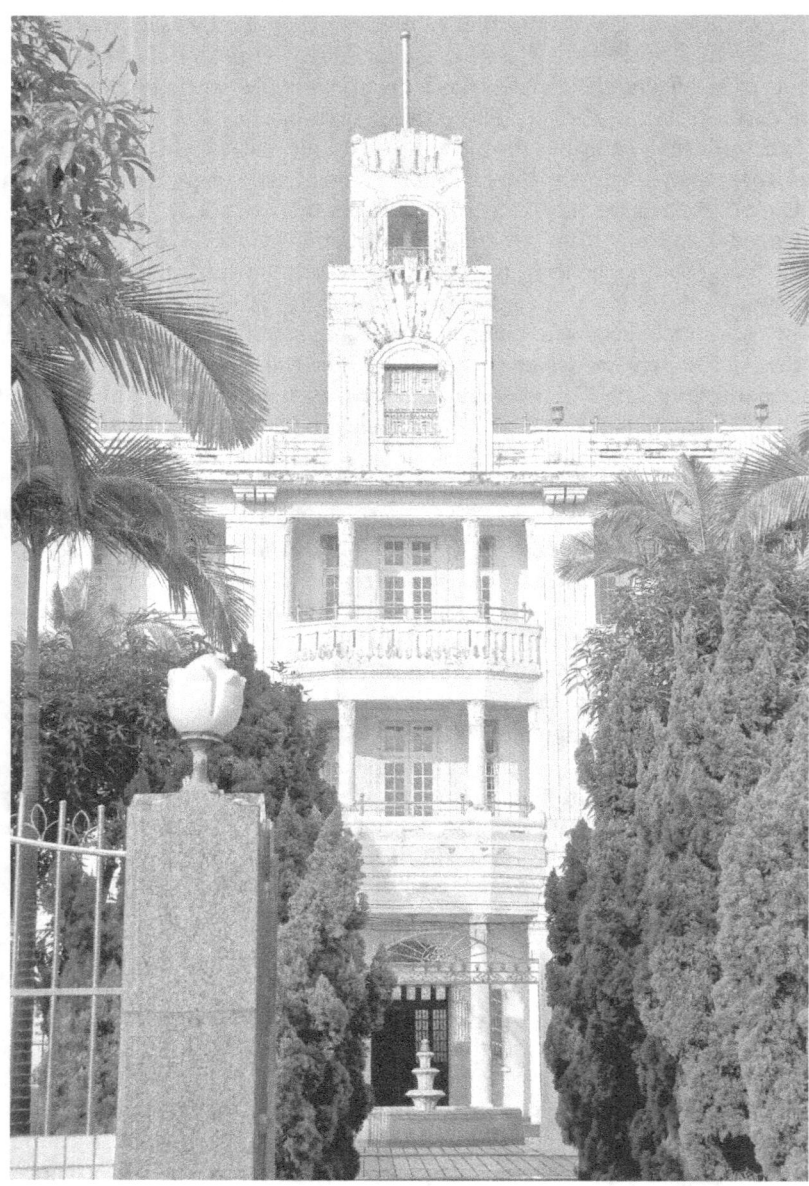

Figure 3.6 Art Deco mansion built by the Kwok brothers in Heng Mei village after their return to Hong Kong from Australia.

in Hong Kong, Shanghai and some other Chinese cities in the first half of the 20th century had their origins in the business activities of men from Zhongshan who migrated to Sydney in the last decades of the 19th century and became successful fruit and vegetable traders there (Chan 1996; Fitzgerald 2007: 190–99). The Sincere and Wing On companies modelled their department stories on the modern style and modern retailing strategy of the large Anthony Hordern & Sons department store that was located only a few blocks from Sydney's Chinatown (Fitzgerald 2007: 194).

The Ma family mansion in Hengmei was in keeping with the style of the family's neoclassical mansion in Hong Kong (now demolished), whereas the Kwok mansion reflected the Art Deco style of the Wing On company's 21-storey apartment block in Shanghai, Wing On Mansions (Denison and Ren 2008: 181). Both houses have large ground floor reception rooms and numerous bedrooms and bathrooms on the floors above, equipped with modern plumbing. They have reinforced concrete frames and floor plates and dispense with gables in favour of flat reinforced concrete roofs. Wall paintings are conspicuously absent, and there is an almost studied avoidance of traditional referents in general, something that may be partly explained by their builders having converted to Christianity while in Australia. The exception is where they reimported Chinese design in the form of European Art Deco motifs that had absorbed 'Chinese' design elements, as seen in the case of the Kwok mansion's internal glass doors with their lattice screen pattern and in the pagoda in the stained glass panel above one of the doors (Figure 3.7). The Chinese influence on Art Deco continued a pattern set by the Art Nouveau movement of the late 1800s and early 1900s (Lancaster 1952).

Art Deco, which was also a design influence in some Type 3 houses, was as transnationally mobile and adaptive as the migrant actors who deployed it in Zhongshan. As Vandana Baweja (2015: 6) observes of Art Deco, 'as it spread across the globe it absorbed and synthesized various geographical and temporal influences that included ancient Egyptian, German modernist, Streamlining, Mayan, Aztec, Babylonian, and African.' The 'aerodynamic aesthetic' of architectural streamlining discussed by Baweja (2015: 6) in relation to Art Deco buildings in Bombay and other Indian cities emerged out of the enthusiasm for speed that gripped many people in the early decades of the 20th century as ever faster motorcars, airplanes and ships came into use. It had a particular resonance for those diaspora Chinese of the Pearl River Delta who, as mentioned earlier, had modern ocean liners depicted in wall paintings in houses they built in their home villages. In practical terms, these new steamships dramatically reduced travel time between migrant origin and destination locales. Their speed was depicted in the paintings by horizontal streams of smoke trailing out from the ships' funnels (Figure 5.2). At the same time, the paintings were a status claim on the part of owners and

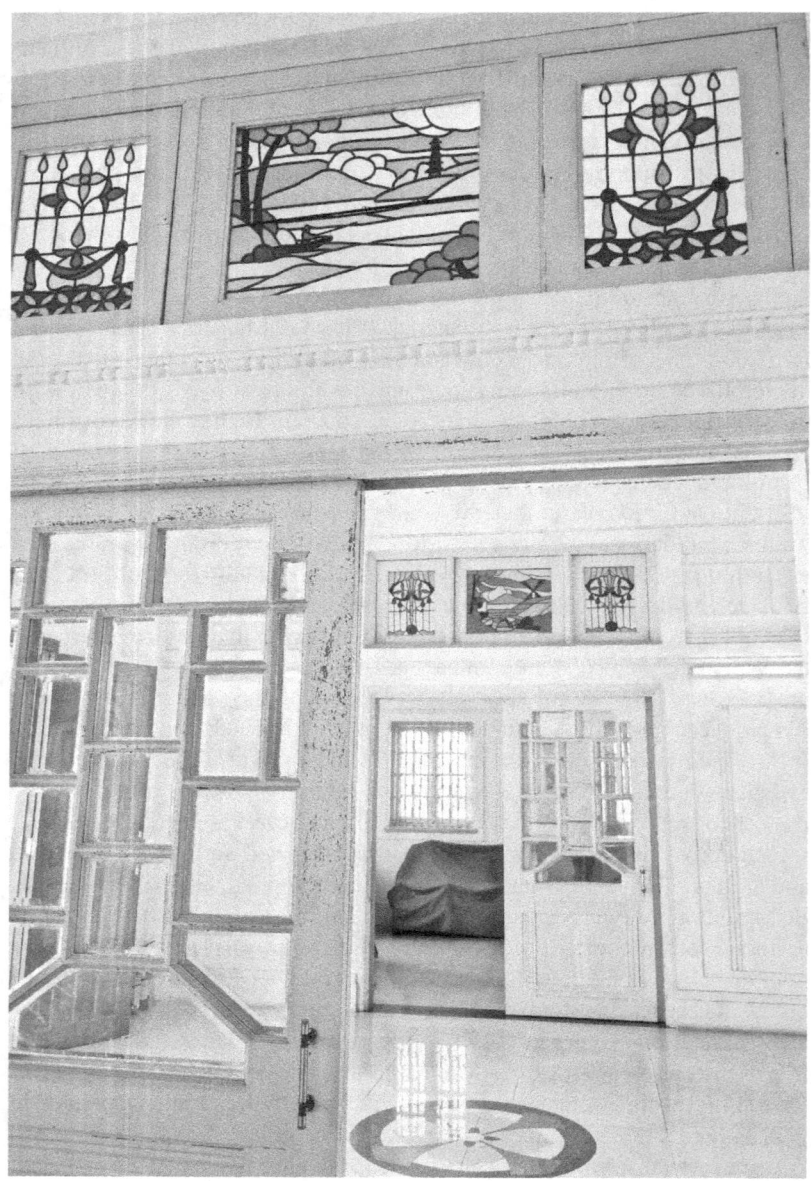

Figure 3.7 Ground floor of Kwok mansion, showing 'lattice screen' style doors and a stained glass window (top centre) featuring a pagoda and a man fishing from a sampan.

occupants of the houses, announcing their belonging to the modern world of international travel. Their equivalent in today's world includes the remittance houses in the Punjab that have large models of jumbo jets mounted on their roofs (Taylor 2015: 200). As a heritage object, the remittance house is a placeholder in the local landscape for the absent (or only occasionally present) migrant, but it also gives material substance and support to new identities being constructed around claims to wealth, social status, cosmopolitanism and global connectivity.

For all their grandeur, the mansions were infrequently occupied, family members being kept busy running their businesses in Hong Kong and Shanghai. Like the department stores themselves, the houses were the acme of modernity. They were dramatic expressions of wealth and status but critically, along with the modern schools endowed by these families in their ancestral villages (Cheng 2020), they were material expressions of the continued importance placed on maintaining ties to the ancestral place and membership of that place's in-situ and diasporic community. Other members of the Ma family had similar, though smaller houses in Hengmei village, and more distant lines of the same lineage who had also sent migrants to Australia built Type 1 and 2 remittance houses there. By employing hundreds of fellow villagers in their department stores in Canton, Hong Kong and Shanghai, the Ma and Kwok families helped network clanspeople from these villages into their business empires (Fitzgerald 2007 199).

The mansions were requisitioned by the Japanese during their 1937–1945 occupation of Guangdong and after 1949 were appropriated to the state by the communist government under Mao, ownership later being restored to the Ma and Kwok families based in Hong Kong and elsewhere outside China's then borders.[7] Now protected as heritage properties, the mansions are a source of pride for family descendants, including those in Australia, and are fixtures of the itineraries of those Zhongshan migrants and their descendants in Australia who make return visits to Zhongshan.[8] Many Zhongshanese in Australia continued to hold shares in the Four Great Companies into the late 20th century. The mansion houses are attention-grabbing objects in the China–Australia heritage corridor, the equivalent, say, of the tower houses built by overseas Chinese in Kaiping County (Figure 3.8), but in terms of providing a well-rounded survey of remittance house types in Zhongshan, they are no more significant than the other houses covered here.

An unstable legacy: migrant houses in the Mao era and beyond

A fundamental tenet of Maoist policy from the 1950s until Mao's death in 1976 was prioritisation of industrial growth. A necessary entailment of this was a rigid

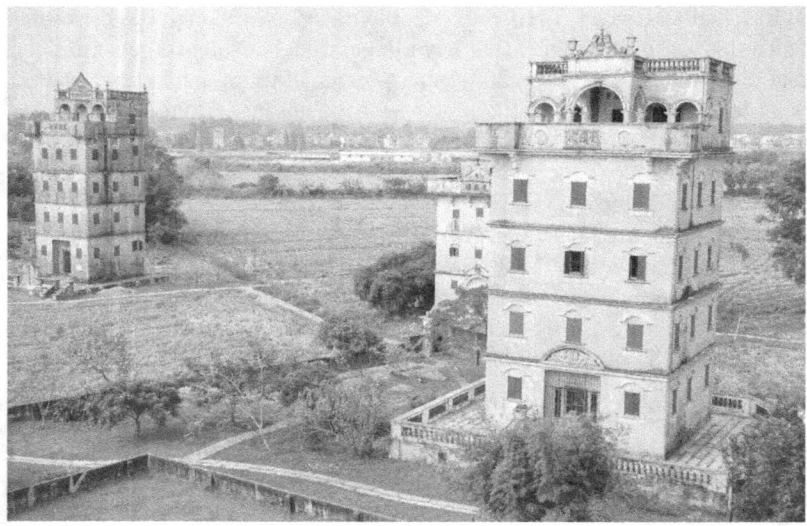

Figure 3.8 Watchtower houses (*diaolou*) in Zili village, Kaiping County, Guangdong.

regime of food extraction from the countryside (Ash 2006: 982). With heavy industry concentrated in the cities, rural areas were given over almost exclusively to food production. Even emigrant areas of the Pearl River Delta, such as Zhongshan, which over the several previous decades had achieved a level of prosperity and modernity in some ways comparable to cities such as Canton and Shanghai, were transformed to conditions concomitant with a near-subsistence peasant economy. Where the foreign connections and remittance income of the families of overseas Chinese had once been the envy of other villagers, now, particularly with the onset of the Korean War in June 1950, the taint of foreignness that such ties carried put these families at great political risk. And where remittances had once allowed them to leave the fields, Maoism sent them back there.

Land that had been purchased by overseas Chinese and their village-based relatives had elevated their social status in the pre-1949 era, but it left them dangerously exposed during the land reform campaign of 1949–1953. Labelled as members of the landlord class, many were executed. Up to 90 percent of all overseas Chinese families in Guangdong suffered confiscation of their houses (Peterson 2012: 52). Houses that once provoked pride or envy in the 1950s and 1960s now intimated bourgeois decadence and counter-revolutionary leanings. By the end of the 20th century, the pendulum had swung back; in official heritage discourse, the houses were now celebrated as a proud legacy of Zhongshan's history of diasporic connections.

However, few of the houses suffered serious damage during the Mao era. Those confiscated during land reform were distributed to villagers classed as poor peasants and landless labourers, the larger houses accommodating multiple families. Some were used as government offices or for other public purposes. Very few new houses were constructed during this period, meaning that when the death of Mao and the downfall of the Gang of Four in 1976 was followed by economic liberalisation, an enormous surge of house construction swept through China. In Fujian, for example, a third of all rural households constructed new houses at this time (Knapp 1996: 782; see also Kuah-Pearce 2008: 124). In Zhongshan, the neoclassicism of the pre-1949 remittance houses gave way to freestyle concrete construction in the pattern of what has come to be called Third World Modernism (Lu 2011). In the emigrant villages, these houses typically form a band around the periphery of the old village core where the pre-1940s remittance houses, temples and lineage halls are concentrated.

The mainland's border with Hong Kong, largely unregulated until 1949, had been closed in the 1950s, giving material form to the Cold War term, the Bamboo Curtain. Yet from then until the late 1970s thousands of mainlanders, including many from Zhongshan, managed to get across to Hong Kong. Many swam across or drowned trying to. The Bamboo Curtain that was drawn across the China–Australia migration corridor in those decades was removed and when traffic along it resumed, the remittance landscape of Zhongshan had for overseas Chinese assumed an aspect of a 'pastness' (see Chapter 1) that it had not had before.

Notes

1 Sandoval-Cervantes' reference here is to Appadurai's *The Future as Cultural Fact* (2013).
2 For an account of the vernacular house in China, see Knapp's *Chinese Houses* (2006).
3 Interview with Jian-Bo Gan, Zhongshan, 9 May 2018.
4 Reverse painting on glass was a decorative art that developed in the context of China's trade with the West in the 18th and 19th centuries but was then absorbed into the domestic market for decorative arts, particularly in coastal China (Howard 1997).
5 For Kaiping *diaolou*, see the UNESCO World Heritage list, https://whc.unesco.org/en/list/1112/, accessed August 2019.
6 Interviews with migrant descendants in Zhongshan and Australia attest to the involvement of architects in the design of some of these houses.

7 Hong Kong Island and the Kowloon peninsula were ceded to Britain in 1842 and 1860, respectively. In 1898, Britain extended the Crown Colony by obtaining a 99-year lease from the Qing government.
8 Information from interviews conducted with Zhongshan migrants and migrant descendants in NSW.

References

Ahmed, Sara. 2006. *Queer Phenomenology: Orientations, Objects, Others*. Durham, NC: Duke University Press.

Appadurai, Arjun. 2013. *The Future as Cultural Fact: Essays on the Global Condition*. Brooklyn, NY: Verso.

Ash, Robert. 2006. 'Squeezing the peasants, grain extraction, food consumption and rural living standards in Mao's China,' *The China Quarterly* 188: 959–198, https://doi.org/10.1017/S0305741006000518.

Baweja, Vandana. 2015. 'Messy modernisms: Otto Koenigsberger's early work in princely Mysore, 1939–41,' *South Asian Studies* 31(1): 1–26, https://doi.org/10.1080/02666030.2015.1008806.

Chan, Anita, Richard Madsen and Jonathan Unger. 2009. *Chen Village: Revolution to Globalization*, third edition. Berkeley: University of California Press, https://doi.org/10.2307/3116879.

Chan, Wellington K. K. 1996. 'Personal styles, cultural values and management: The Sincere and Wing On companies in Shanghai and Hong Kong,' *The Business History Review* 40: 141–166.

Chan-Yeung, Moira M. W. 2017. *Lam Woo: Master Builder, Revolutionary, and Philanthropist*. Hong Kong: Chinese University of Hong Kong Press.

Cheng, Christopher. 2020. 'Beacons of modern learning: Diaspora-funded schools in the China-Australia corridor,' *Asian and Pacific Migration Journal* 29(2): 139–162, https://doi.org/10.1177/0117196820930309.

Cook, James A. 2008. 'Reimagining China: Xiamen, overseas Chinese, and a transnational modernity,' in Madeleine Yue Dong and Joshua Lewis Goldstein (eds.), *Everyday Modernity in China*, pp. 156–194. Seattle: University of Washington Press.

Dalakoglou, Dimitris. 2010. 'Migrating-remitting-"building"-dwelling: House-making as "proxy" presence in postsocialist Albania,' *The Journal of the Royal Anthropological Institute* 16(4): 761–777, https://doi.org/10.1111/j.1467-9655.2010.01652.x.

Denison, Edward. 2017. *Architecture and the Landscape of Modernity in China Before 1949*. Abingdon, UK: Routledge, https://doi.org/10.4324/9781315567686.

Denison, Edward and Guang Yu Ren. 2008. *Modernism in China: Architectural Visions and Revolutions*. London: Wiley.

DeSilvey, Caitlin and Rodney Harrison. 2020. 'Anticipating loss: Rethinking endangerment in heritage futures,' *International Journal of Heritage Studies* 26(1): 1–7, https://doi.org/10.1080/13527258.2019.1644530

Dikötter, Frank. 2007. *Things Modern: Material Culture and Everyday Life in China*. London: Hurst.

Farris, Johnathan A. 2007. *Enclave to Urbanity: Canton, Foreigners, and Architecture from Late Eighteenth to the Early Nineteenth Centuries*. Hong Kong: Hong Kong University Press.

Fitzgerald, John. 2007. *Big White Lie: Chinese Australians in White Australia*. Sydney: University of New South Wales Press.

Fredheim, L. Harold and Manal Khalaf. 2016. 'The significance of values: Heritage value typologies re-examined,' *International Journal of Heritage Studies* 22(6): 466–481, https://doi.org/10.1080/13527258.2016.1171247.

Hosagrahar, Jyoti. 2005. *Indigenous Modernities: Negotiating Architecture and Urbanism*. London: Routledge.

Howard, David S. 1997. *A Tale of Three Cities: Canton, Shanghai & Hong Kong. Three Centuries of Sino-British Trade in the Decorative Arts*. London: Sotheby's.

Knapp, Ronald G. 1996. 'Rural housing and village transformation in Taiwan and Fujian,' *China Quarterly* 147: 779–794, https://doi.org/10.1017/S0305741000051791.

Knapp, Ronald G. 2006. *Chinese Houses: The Heritage of a Nation*. Tokyo: Tuttle.

Kourelis, Kostis. 2020. 'Three Elenis: Archaeologies of the Greek American village home,' *Journal of Modern Greek Studies* 38(1): 85–108.

Kuah-Pearce, Khun Eng. 2008. 'Collective memories as cultural capital: From Chinese diaspora to emigrant hometowns,' in Khun Eng Kuah-Pearce and Andrew P. Davidson (eds.), *At Home in the Chinese Diaspora: Memories, Identities and Belongings*, pp. 111–127. New York: Palgrave Macmillan.

Lancaster, Clay. 1952. 'Oriental contributions to Art Nouveau,' *The Art Bulletin* 34: 297–310.

Lu, Duanfang (ed.). 2011. *Third World Modernism: Architecture, Development and Identity*. London: Routledge.

McKeown, Adam. 2001. *Chinese Migrant Networks and Cultural Change: Peru, Chicago, Hawaii, 1900–1936*. Chicago: University of Chicago Press.

Peterson, Glen. 2012. *Overseas Chinese in the People's Republic of China*. London: Routledge.

Sandoval-Cervantes, Iván. 2017. 'Uncertain futures: The unfinished houses of undocumented migrants in Oaxaca, Mexico,' *American Anthropologist* 119(2): 209–222, https://doi.org/10.1111/aman.12864.

Taylor, Steve. 2015. ' "Home is never fully achieved . . . even when we are in it": Migration, belonging and social exclusion within Punjabi transnational mobility,' *Mobilities* 10: 193–210, https://doi.org/10.1080/17450101.2013.848606.

Tsin, Michael. 2001. 'Canton remapped,' in Joseph W. Esherick (ed.), *Remaking the Chinese City: Modernity and National Identity, 1900–1950*, pp. 19–29. Honolulu: University of Hawai'i Press.

Williams, Michael. 2018. *Returning Home with Glory: Chinese Villagers Around the Pacific, 1849 to 1949*. Hong Kong: Hong Kong University Press.

Wong, Pamela Lee. 2018. *The Mystery Aussie Jan See Chin*. Palo Alto, CAL: PWL Publishing.

Zhu, Xiaoyang. 2014. *Topography of Politics in Rural China: The Story of Xiaocun*. Singapore: World Scientific Publishing.

4 Venerable ancestors and seagoing gods

Over the century or so before 1940, the period in which what is often referred to as the 'first wave' of Chinese migration to Western countries took place, Chinese religion was often seen as modernity's other. Christian missionaries and colonial officials in Asia tended to denounce Chinese religion as pure superstition, maintaining that 'idol' worship was both useless and evil and that the West's technological and economic superiority was clear evidence of Christianity's superiority. For their part, Asian elites argued that indigenous religion, steeped in the supernatural, was an obstacle to the establishment of technologically and economically modern nation-states that could stand up to Western hegemony (Goossaert 2006; Yang 2004). But most Chinese migrants seem to have regarded their religious practice as perfectly compatible with modern life.

While some Chinese migrants in the pre-1949 era may have adhered to a purer form of Buddhism or Taoism, the vast majority of those who were not Christian converts were followers of a popular form of Chinese religion that was an amalgam of Taoism, Buddhism, ancestor worship and the cults of an extensive pantheon of popular gods, many of whom were localised to the migrants' origin places. As this chapter will show, the religious practices and religious material culture of Chinese migrants circulated between these places and their destination locales, bringing into being a translocal religious landscape.

In what follows, the role of religion in migration, and by extension its place in the heritage of migration, is illustrated firstly by reference to the way Chinese migrants in Southeast Asia and elsewhere have related to the landscape of their adoptive country by merging their religious beliefs and practices with the existing sacred topography they entered. The role of incense and the 'division of incense' as a means of establishing the presence of Chinese gods in destination locales is described. By way of comparison, consideration is also given to the way the topography of Christianity has been geographically extended via colonialism. The discussion then turns to consider the Chinese

DOI: 10.4324/9781003088714-5

lineage in the context of migrancy, looking particularly at the implications of ancestor worship for the material heritage record. Attention is given to lineage halls and the involvement of diasporic lineage members in their restoration. I then consider ways in which overseas Chinese are 'presenced' in their home villages by religious means, particularly via donations made to temple and ancestral hall restoration projects.

Chinese migration and the sacramental landscape

The localisation of the divine is one of the characteristics of indigenous religions in Asia, whether taking the form of offerings made to the spirits of sacred rocks and trees by Thai Buddhists (Gesick 1995: 69; Munier 1998), belief in the miraculous efficacy of water emanating from sacred springs at Chinese temples (Chau 2005), or of a sacred mountain in the Philippines reproducing the miraculous landscape of Calvary (Gorospe 1992). The role that this topographic aspect of religion has played in human migration has a deep history.

At face value, there may seem something contradictory in the assertion that the topographic groundedness of Chinese 'popular religion',[1] a characteristic that inevitably binds people to their home terrain, can aid migrants in adapting to and integrating themselves with the landscapes they migrate to. In resolving this, it may help to consider some specific examples from the history of Chinese migration to Southeast Asia, which began in the 15th century following the Ming admiral Zheng He's voyages of exploration and intensified from about 1700. In China, a key component of popular religion in the home villages and counties of these migrants are the topographic cults centred on spirits and deities that are anchored to specific locales, such as fields, crossroads, springs, hills and trees. This sacred landscape is clearly not transferable. Migrants leave it behind them, but studies of the religiosity of Chinese in Southeast Asia show that they have taken with them there a belief (or openness to the idea) that foreign lands are likely to be populated by generically similar deities and supernatural forces to those they knew at home. They take with them what Naquin and Yu (1992: 22) refer to as a belief in the 'intrinsic numinosity of nature.'

The anthropologist William Newell (1962) described such a situation in the hinterland of Butterworth, on the northwest Malay Peninsula, opposite the island of Penang, where he carried out ethnographic fieldwork in the 1950s. Migrant farmers from the Teochew-speaking Shantou region in north-eastern Guangdong had established themselves in the area some decades previously. They built simple, rustic temples and open-sided corrugated iron shelters for the popular gods they brought with them from Shantou, as represented in their statues, but they also honoured local indigenous spirits whose existence they discovered when carving fields out of the scrub to grow sugar cane and rice. They began making offerings to trees that were sacred to the Malay people of the area and also made offerings at shrines to Malay tutelary spirits (*keramat*), many of which are believed to mark the burial places of historically important Muslim saints (Mandal 2012). According to Newell, the Chinese regarded *keramat* as the equivalent of their earth gods back in Shantou (Newell 1962: 99), but since they were Malay spirits, they were conceived by the Chinese to be Muslim and thus needing to be propitiated with offerings other than pork. A similar situation can be witnessed today on the small island of Pulau Ubin, in the Johor Strait which divides Singapore from Malaysia. I have observed *keramat* being worshiped there alongside Chinese gods in the small rustic shrines erected by Chinese migrants who worked the island's granite quarries in the 19th and 20th centuries (Figure 4.1). The statues of these *keramat* have dark complexions and wear traditional Malay headdress and clothing. They are hybrid deities, the equivalent of the Datuk-Kong place-guardians found in shrines at the entrance to Chinese neighbourhoods, temples and houses in Malaysia (Widodo 2016: 85).

The willingness of Chinese migrants to recognise and propitiate these objects of Malay animistic worship attests to the existence of what Beng-Lan

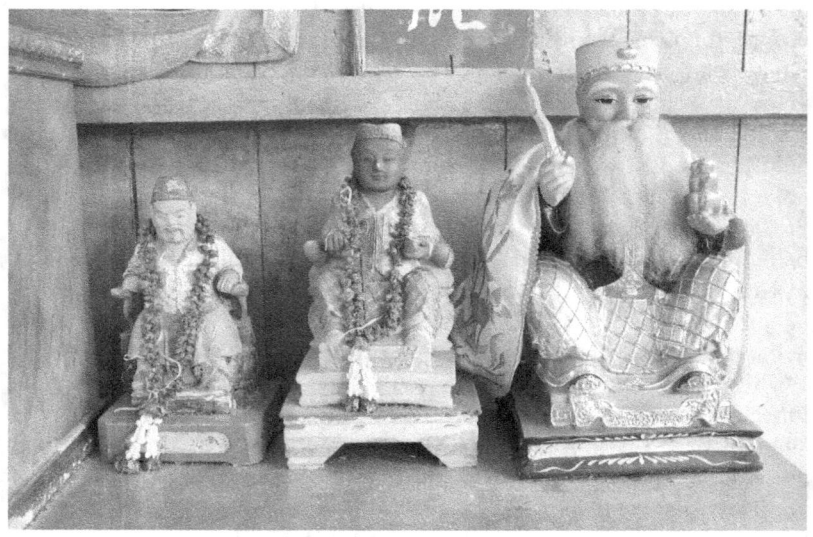

Figure 4.1 Statues of two Malay deities (*keramat*), on the left, share an altar shelf with Caishen, the Chinese god of wealth (right), Pulau Ubin, Singapore.

Goh (2011: 145) refers to as 'transethnic cosmologies'. Goh's research in urban settings on Penang Island indicates that the openness of Chinese migrants to the Malay sacramental topography is not confined to rural landscapes. All of the 20 Chinese construction companies in his Penang study propitiated the *keramat* of their building sites with halal food offerings, having set up temporary or, in a few cases, permanent on-site shrines to them (see also Cheu 1996: 9). Goh (2011: 156) remarks that, with the 'increasing conservatism and bureaucratization' of Islam in Malaysia since the 1980s, ethnic Chinese and Indian Malaysians have gradually taken over from Muslims in the worship of *keramat*.

Jean Debernardi (2004), in her long-term ethnography of immigrant Chinese religion on Penang, describes how in the late 18th century the spirit of a Chinese pioneer migrant, Chang Li, who was killed by a falling boulder, became Tua Pek Kong, the God of Prosperity for Chinese in Penang. A temple was built to him on the island in 1799. Tua Pek Kong's identity 'has fused with his new land' (Debernardi 2004: 151) and his worship has come to resemble elements of Malay animism: 'The syncretic convergence is suggested by Chang Li's death by a boulder, for Malay Datuk Keramat often die by a sacred stone or transform into a stone on death' (Debernardi 2004: 152). As Cristina Rocha puts it, 'new sacred assemblages can latch on to older ones' (Rocha 2020: 213), a tendency that characterises transnational religious flows in the context of migration. In their worship of the syncretic deity, Tua Pek Kong, Chinese entrepreneurs in Penang have extended 'recognition and respect to the original spiritual protectors of the land that yielded them great wealth' (Debernardi 2004: 152). The grounding of Chinese religion in the local terrain of Penang also saw temples built in mountain caves and propitious positions close to the island's shore (Debernardi 2004: 43).

Newell (1962: 99) makes the point that in the Teochew homeland of north-eastern Guangdong, it was believed that if a farming family migrated, its ancestors, materialised in the form of ancestral tablets, moved with them while the earth god stayed behind to be worshipped by the farmer taking up the emigrant family's fields. The Chinese gods they worshipped in the new country were a combination of gods local to their homeland counties and various major gods of the Chinese pantheon. Statues of both categories of god were carried with the original migrants or brought by those returning from home visits. There are also situations in which gods appear in new locales of their own volition – witness the temples to the goddess Mazu, the Empress of Heaven (Tin Hau in Cantonese), in Hong Kong that commonly have origin myths describing a statue of the goddess washing up on the beach and becoming a community's patron deity (Liu 2003: 378).

One of the principal ways that Chinese gods follow their living devotees as they migrate, taking up 'real presence' in the destination landscape, is via the phenomenon of 'divided incense' (*fenxiang*). Ash from the urn of a god's temple is believed to be imbued with its *ling* (efficacious power) and thus to be a miraculously potent substance in its own right (Habkirk and Chang 2017; Feuchtwang 2001: 138). Hence, when a portion of the ash is taken from an incense urn at a temple where a particular god has demonstrated its efficacious power, usually by granting favours, and transported to the urn of a newly established branch temple, the deity's presence is replicated there. A branch temple, in turn, can seed offspring temples (also known as daughter temples) in a process that creates chains of subsidiary temples linking back to temples on the Chinese mainland (Habkirk and Chang 2017: 165–166).

Praying to a god in a temple where the deity's presence has not been established in this intensely material way would be a useless exercise, whether that temple is in China, Penang, Sydney or London, because the god is not present there. Whereas, once its presence is established there by means of the material thread of 'incense genealogy' (Habkirk and Chang 2017: 170), its miraculous efficacy can be summoned up at temples anywhere in the geographic diaspora the deity's devotees happen to be.

The colonial context

Not all migrant destination locales have been as amenable to the practice of Chinese popular religion as those mentioned earlier. And when it comes to long-distance religious flows, these have also occurred in the situation of colonialism. During the Spanish conquest and colonisation of America, for example, Christian crosses were erected and churches built on many sacred sites of the Aztec and other indigenous peoples. In this process of substitution, the Spanish implicitly acknowledged the principle that if divine power was manifest at particular locations in the landscape of Spain, it could equally be manifest in the New World, both places being within God's universe. Statues of the Virgin erected at such New World sites, including those of Our Lady of Los Remedios, quickly exhibited miraculous powers and became objects of pilgrimage (Brading 2001: 46–47), seeming thus to fulfil the Spanish 'dream' that the devotion of the Indians for their idols and deities would be transferred to Christ (Greenblatt 1991: 138).

Mexican migrants to the USA have taken the worship of the Virgin of Guadalupe along with them, establishing a terrain of sacred Guadalupan sites in areas where they have settled (Pena 2011). Some of these sites attract pilgrimages, while, at the same time, devotees of the Virgin travel on pilgrimages, often in groups, back from the USA to Mexico City where the 'original' of her statue is located. Similarly, transnational pilgrimage networks link the origin shrine of the Chinese goddess Mazu, located on Meizhou Island in China's Zhejiang Province, to devotees in Taiwan, California, Indonesia and elsewhere (Yang 2008). The flow of people and objects, including amulets and other religious paraphernalia, along transnational pilgrimage routes parallels, or is incorporated in, the flows that occur along migration corridors. A characteristic of pilgrimage networks is that the origin site of a cult is generally believed to possess more divine power than subsidiary sites, leading, for example, to the situation common to Chinese popular religion in which statues of gods from diaspora-situated shrines are carried back across transborder space by sea, or these days by airplane, to the origin temple in order to have their divine efficacy 'recharged' there.

It is interesting to compare the situation of Chinese migrants in Australia with that of their counterparts in Penang (Debernardi 2004) and the hinterland of Butterworth (Newell 1962) where, as shown, there was fusion and interplay between the religion migrants brought with them and the indigenous sacramental landscape they settled in. In Australia, Aboriginal religion is centred on the Dreaming, a dynamic spiritual realm in which ancestral spirits form the terrain of mountains, streams, rocks, waterholes and other topographic features, and in which people have an embodied relationship with these spirits (Charlesworth, Dussart and Morphy 2005). There is no evidence of Chinese migrants in Australia having engaged directly with the Aboriginal religious topography of the storied sites of ancestral spirit beings. However, given that Chinese men and Aboriginal women frequently formed romantic-sexual partnerships (Jones 2005; Ramsay 2003), it is not unlikely this occurred.

For their part, European colonists in Australia, whether Protestant or Catholic, regarded the Australian landscape as religiously a blank slate, a tabula rasa they set out to populate with churches, chapels and the consecrated ground of cemeteries (Byrne et al. 2006). Rather than engaging with a landscape in which divine force was seen to be immanent, they approached the terrain of Australia via the rationalist discourse of natural history (including botany, geology and biology) and the scientific technology of resource mapping. By contrast, Chinese migrants in Australia brought with them the science of geomancy or *feng shui*, practiced by Chinese in all their countries of residence. In the Australian context, Gordon Waitt describes the 'psychological' significance of *feng shui* as a practice that 'generates feelings of familiarity' for Chinese migrants in their new country (Waitt 2003: 229).

White settlers had already dispossessed Aboriginal people of their land by the time the Chinese arrived in the areas where they settled. And by the time the Chinese began arriving in significant numbers in the mid-19th century, white settlers already heavily outnumbered Aboriginal people. In colonial Malaya, however, Malays always vastly outnumbered white colonials, and the Malay religious topography was consequently more 'available' to Chinese migrants than it was in Australia.

Ancestral halls and their diasporic congregations

Lineages organised as corporate bodies gained importance in southern China during the Ming Dynasty (1368–1644). By the 16th century in the Pearl River Delta, the origin place of most Chinese migrants to North America and Australia, lineages were deeply engaged in building up their estates (Faure 2007: 125). By the 19th century, population pressure in the Delta region was such that overseas migration had become a popular option for young men, particularly for younger sons. Rather than being compromised by the spatial dispersion of its members, keeping the estate intact and in place could at times actually require dispersion (Kuhn 2008: 15). Those who migrated remitted a significant part of their income back home to their family and lineage, allowing lineages to build or renovate temples, ancestral halls and schools. The emigrant village in southern China became a 'transnational entity' (McKeown 2001: 75).

The elaborate traditional architecture and the age of many ancestral halls in southern China have earned them a place on the heritage inventories of county or provincial-level governments, but this has little significance in isolation from what occurs inside these buildings and what, indeed, they embody. On ritual occasions, the ancestors are believed to take up a presence in the halls, which function as liminal portals between the terrestrial and heavenly worlds, much the way graves in China are thought of as liminal gateways between the two realms (Rawson 1996). While, spatially, many lineages have been stretched by transnational migration, in their temporal dimension, they extend across past, present and future generations (Lakos 2010). In the act of ancestor worship, a lineage's membership is called together across time and space in a way that dissolves national boundaries and in a sense cancels out the physical remoteness of overseas migrants. The border-transcending capacity of ancestor worship is key to understanding how it has supported migration and to appreciating why homeland ancestral halls attract overseas lineage members with a kind of gravitational force.

Over most of the Pearl River Delta area, single lineage villages such as that of San Tin, described in Chapter 2 were common. The primary material site and anchor of the lineage was its ancestral hall, traditionally the most prominent building in the village. The halls have the high gable roofs covered with glazed terracotta tiles and the upturned eaves that we associate with traditional Chinese architecture. The roof frame is supported in front by a row of granite columns beyond which a portico leads to a large central hall at the far end of which, prior to 1949, was an altar upon which were arranged the wooden ancestral tablets of the deceased males, often including those who died overseas. Today, migrant lineage members, living and dead, are given presence in the halls by having their names inscribed in the genealogical record book and on genealogical charts that are often hung on the walls. But the halls are not mere venues for ancestor worship and genealogical record keeping, they are part of the lineage's very substance (Liu 1995). Lineages in southern China can be thought of as temporal–spatial assemblages, or 'imbroglios' (Latour 2007: 46), comprising their living and deceased members, the agricultural land of their members and the ancestral halls, temples, ancestral graves and ancestral tablets that belong to them. The progressive decay of the halls, accentuated by the delta's humid subtropical climate, provides the occasion for lineage members to collaborate in undertaking restoration projects, a collective action that reinforces the lineage as a social unit.

Following the founding of the Peoples Republic in 1949, all lineage lands in southern China were confiscated and divided among tenant farmers (Siu 2016: 152), and the lineages ceased to exist as political entities. However, in the four decades since Mao's death in 1976, several ancestral halls in the emigrant villages of Zhongshan have undergone major restorations, funded in significant part by lineage members living in Hong Kong or other parts of China and by the overseas diaspora. A recent example is the hall of the Choy lineage in Waisha village, situated today in the Zhuhai Special Economic Zone. During the commune era, beginning in 1958, the Choy ancestral hall was turned into a communal dining hall and when the communes were disbanded in the 1970s it was left in a state of dereliction. By 2014, a tree had taken root in the hall and was growing through a space where the roof had fallen in.

This situation lasted until several years ago when a small number of the clan's male elders launched a restoration drive, sending out a call for donations to lineage members living away from Waisha. The enthusiastic response led to a team of professional ancestral hall and temple restorers being contracted to carry out the work (Figure 4.2). Roughly half the material fabric of the hall was replaced, including the wooden roof frame, roof tiles and many of the terracotta floor tiles. Salvageable woodwork was refinished. The hall's wall paintings, with their depictions of gods, scenes from legendary stories and auspicious fruit, had deteriorated badly, portions of them being so faded and exfoliated as to be barely legible (Figure 4.3). Some had been covered over with a layer of black stucco cement by iconoclastic Red Guards during the Cultural Revolution (1966–1976) and portions of this were chipped off as carefully as possible by the restoration team.

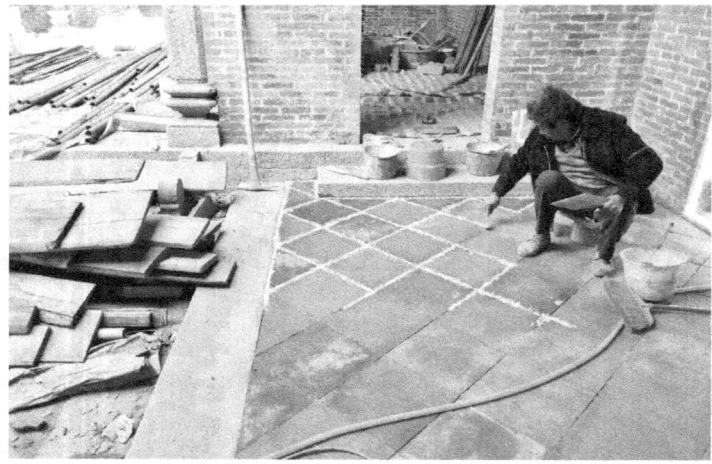

Figure 4.2 Laying new terracotta floor tiles in the Choy ancestral hall, Waisha village, Zhongshan. To the left are wooden planks from the pre-existing structure.

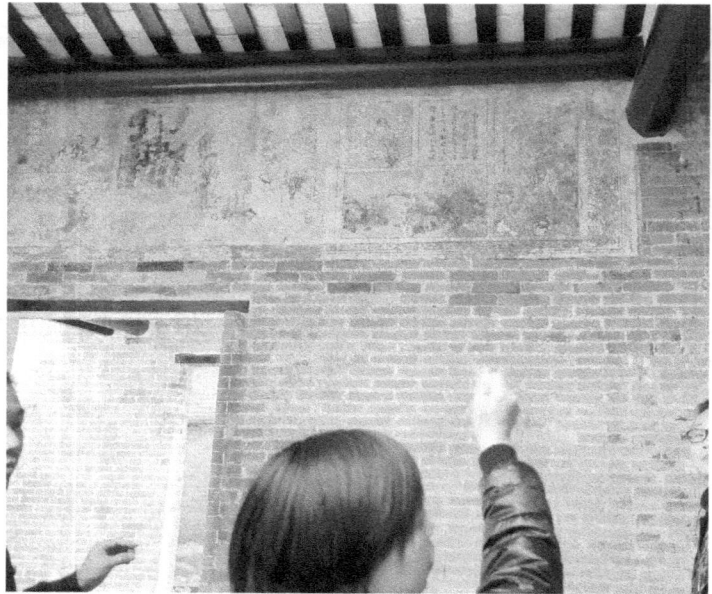

Figure 4.3 Deteriorated wall paintings at the Choy ancestral hall, Waisha village, Zhongshan.

The restoration of the hall was overseen by the prefectural government's heritage experts, under the direction of whom the wall paintings were stabilised in their present state rather than repainted, as some lineage members would have wished. Exemplified here is a tension that has come to exist in many parts of Asia between heritage experts who, adopting a secular-rational approach to religious heritage, regard only the historical elements of such paintings as authentic, and local religious believers who regard the images as embodiments of deities and wish to continue the traditional practice of repainting them as an act of devotion (Byrne 2014: 95–99). In this way, heritage practice confines authenticity to the past. The way the situation was handled in Waisha makes clear that while it is lineages that own the ancestral halls of Zhongshan and pay for their restoration, the government, through its heritage agency, asserts ultimate authority over their management.

The spiritual presence of migrants in their Chinese homeplaces

The lineage in southern China is a social-religious entity. Although a large proportion of the present-day membership of lineages, local and diasporic, have ostensibly renounced belief in Chinese popular religion, with all its attributes of manifest supernatural power that were glossed by modernist reformers as superstition (*mixin* in Chinese), they nevertheless will often still light incense and make other offerings to their ancestors (including those of the preceding few generations). I suggest it is also the case that by participating in restoration projects such as the one described earlier, lineage members almost inevitably engage with the lineage's religious dimension.

It has become common in recent decades for local restoration committees to circulate photos depicting the restoration work among overseas lineage members to keep them informed of progress, reinforcing the diaspora's sense of involvement in the work they are partly paying for. Copies of the photos are often kept on display on a notice board inside the ancestral hall during and after restoration. In earlier times, they were circulated to a limited extent overseas by post; these days they circulate widely via the various forms of digital media that have collapsed the distance between home and away. Details of donations are also broadcast in this way and act as a cross-border accompaniment to the donor plaques that are erected at the lineage hall to permanently record the names and locations of principal donors. Stone-inscribed donor plaques have been a feature of Chinese temples since ancient times (e.g., Wong 2004) and are standard elements of the 'furniture' of ancestral halls, temples and schools in Zhongshan that were built or restored in the 19th and 20th centuries with the involvement of diaspora donors. James Watson (1977: 348) writes that over 600 emigrant members of the Man lineage donated to the 1970s restoration of the Tin Hau temple in their ancestral village. The names of major donors were inscribed in marble, the others having their names displayed on sheets of red paper on show outside the temple during its re-opening.

Donor plaques memorialise not just the donor's financial contribution, they are also long-lasting statements of their belongingness to a lineage and its ancestral hall. In the case of a temple, they serve as a semi-permanent record of a donor's devotion to a particular deity and membership of the deity's cult. Diasporic donors are thus presenced at the site of a temple or lineage hall, a presence frequently also taking material form in the giant red candles, sometimes reaching three or four metres in height, and the large incense coils, both purchased on their behalf by local relatives. The candles and incense will burn continuously for days or even weeks. Incense smoke is traditionally held to be a sacred material in its own right that pervades the interior of a temple and, in rising, reaches and is registered by gods who are sensible to the devotion of their followers and, regardless of where a devotee is located, will provide favours in return.

Family members of emigrants pray for the wellbeing and, often, for the safe return of loved ones overseas. Whether those who have departed have entered their destination countries legally or as undocumented migrants, the act of migration is conceived as an inherently dangerous undertaking (Chu 2010). At a temple in the emigrant village of Caobian, Zhongshan, generations of relatives of emigrants have prayed and made offerings to the goddess Mazu on behalf of family members overseas. A four-metre-long wooden model of a junk under sail stands to the side of the main hall, donated by a villager resident in Hong Kong for members of her family abroad (Figure 4.4). Mazu, popularly believed to have lived on the coast of Fujian Province between 960 and 987 AD, is the tutelary deity of seafarers. She has a massive following in southern China, Taiwan and Southeast Asia and her association with sea travel makes her a particular focus of devotion by migrants and their families.

Where there are sufficient concentrations of migrants of the same lineage overseas, they have sometimes created their own ancestral halls, such as those in the Philippines that take the form of multi-storey clubhouses with an ancestral hall on the top level where offerings are made and prayers said for clan ancestors (See 1981: 233, 238). Similar 'elevated' ancestral halls are found in San Francisco's Chinatown. In Melbourne, migrants from the See Yup region of the Pearl River Delta incorporated chambers in their 1866 temple to Guandi (the god of war) to house more than 13,000 ancestral tablets of men from See Yup who died in Australia (Couchman 2019: 58). In the period prior to World War II, the bones of Chinese settlers and sojourners who died overseas, including in Southeast Asia, Australia, Canada and the USA, were often returned to China for burial in the cemetery of their

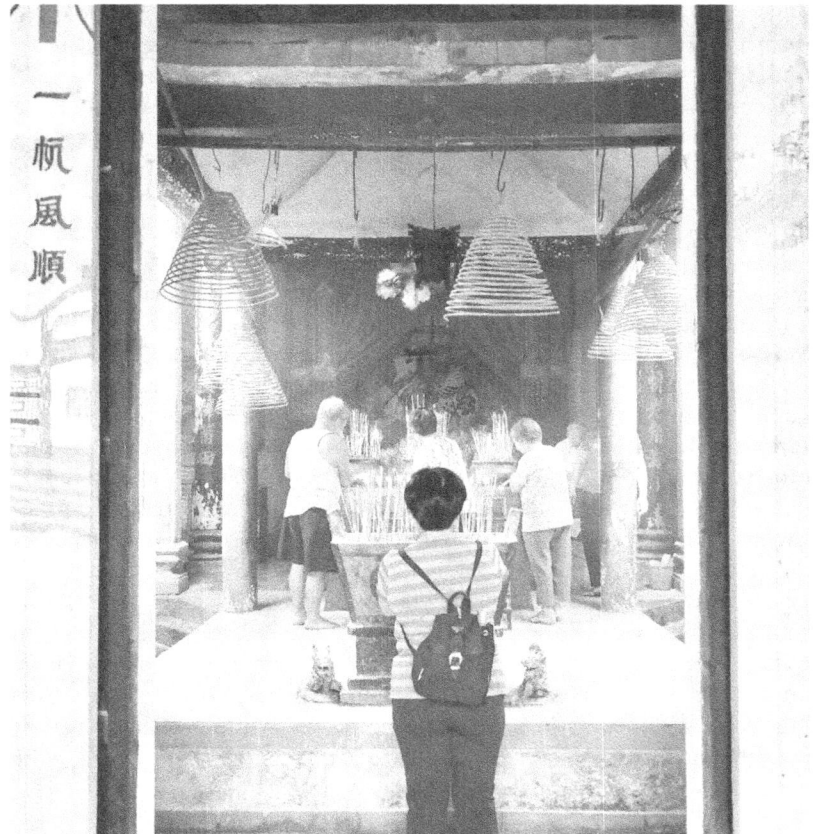

Figure 4.4 The Mazu temple at Caobian village, Zhongshan.

ancestral village.[2] Those destined for native place villages and towns in Guangdong most often went via the Tung Wah Coffin Home in Hong Kong, administered by the Tung Wah Hospital.

Concluding remarks

The centuries-long history of secularisation in the West (Taylor 2007) may encourage a view that religion no longer has a major role to play in global migration. This could not be further from the truth. Since World War II, the great majority of transnational migrants have been those originating in the Global South, most notably in India, China, Africa and Latin America.[3]

There, as also in migrant-sending regions such as Southeast Asia, the Caribbean and the Mediterranean, secularisation has been far less pronounced than in northern Europe, North America and Western outliers like Australia. This, I argue, has meant that religion remains a dynamic force in contemporary migration and that it continues to add to the material record of migration.

Many millions of people across Asia, Latin America, Africa and the European Mediterranean combine their membership of world religions with devotion to a vast array of spirits and deities which lie outside the canonical bounds of these religions. They subscribe to the belief that the miraculous efficacy of extra-canonical spirits and deities is an immanent force in a panoply of objects and places (Chau 2005; Chu 2010; Feuchtwang 2001; Jackson 1999; Moore and Sanders 2001; Rocha and Vásquez 2013). In the foregoing pages, I have attempted to show how belief in divine immanence has played out in the case of Chinese popular religion in migration settings. It remains to say here that such belief is not a fading remnant of traditional religion surviving as an outlier in the modern world but is, rather, a highly dynamic field of belief and practice flourishing under modern conditions of life and eminently mobile in the context of migration. In consequence of this, materialities of religion, saturated with the magical-supernatural, are emergent in migrant destinations, with immense implications for heritage as a field of practice. The introduction of these religious materialities to migrant-receiving countries poses a challenge for a conventional heritage practice in the West which is deeply secular (Byrne 2020). It is unsurprising that, embedded as it is in four centuries of Western cultural history, conventional heritage practice views with suspicion any suggestion that the materiality of religion embodies anything but plain, inert matter.

Notes

1 Popular religion encompasses those beliefs and practices that effectively bypass religious texts and religious professionals to engage directly with spirits and deities via physical manifestations of their presence in the earthly realm and via magic ritual. For Chinese popular religion, see Feuchtwang (2001).
2 Chinese in Northwest America Research Committee, 'Reburial: exhuming the dead and returning them to China,' online publication, www.cinarc.org/Death-2.html.
3 *World Migration Report 2020*. Geneva: International Organization for Migration.

References

Brading, D.A. 2001. *Mexican Phoenix: Our Lady of Guadalupe: Image and Tradition Across Five Centuries*. Cambridge: Cambridge University Press.

Byrne, Denis. 2014. *Counterheritage: Critical Perspectives on Heritage Conservation in Asia*. New York: Routledge.

Byrne, Denis. 2020. 'Divinely significant: Towards a post-secular approach to the materiality of popular religion in Asia,' *International Journal of Heritage Studies* 26(9): 857–873, https://doi.org/10.1080/13527258.2019.1590447.

Byrne, Denis, Heather Goodall, Stephen Wearing and Allison Cadzow. 2006. 'Enchanted parklands,' *Australian Geographer* 37(1): 103–115, https://doi.org/10.1080/00049180500512002.

Charlesworth, Max, Françoise Dussart and Howard Morphy (eds.). 2005. *Aboriginal Religions in Australia: An Anthology of Recent Writings*. Aldershot, UK and Burlington, VT: Ashgate.

Chau, Adam Yuet. 2005. *Miraculous Response: Doing Popular Religion in Contemporary China*. Stanford: Stanford University Press.

Cheu, Hock Tong. 1996. 'Malay keramat, Chinese worshippers: The sinicization of Malay keramats in Malaysia,' Paper 25, Department of Malay Studies, National University of Singapore.

Chu, Julie. 2010. *Cosmologies of Credit: Transnational Mobility and the Politics of Destination in China*. Durham, NC: Duke University Press.

Couchman, Sophie. 2019. 'Melbourne's See Yup Kuan Ti temple: A historical overview,' *Southern Chinese Diaspora Studies* 8: 50–81.

Debernardi, Jean. 2004. *Rites of Belonging: Memory, Modernity, and Identity in a Malaysian Chinese Community*. Stanford: Stanford University Press.

Faure, David. 2007. *Emperor and Ancestor: State and Lineage in South China*. Stanford: Stanford University Press.

Feuchtwang, Stephan. 2001. *Popular Religion in China: The Imperial Metaphor*. London and New York: Routledge.

Gesick, Lorraine M. 1995. *In the Land of Lady White Blood*. Ithaca, NY: Southeast Asia Program, Cornell University.

Goh, Beong-Lan. 2011. 'Spirit cults and construction sites: Trans-ethnic popular religion and Keramat symbolism in contemporary Malaysia,' in Kirsten W. Endres and Andrea Lauser (eds.), *Engaging the Spirit World: Popular Beliefs and Practices in Modern Southeast Asia*, pp. 144–162. New York and Oxford: Berghahn.

Goossaert, Vincent. 2006. '1898: The beginning of the end for Chinese religion?' *Journal of Asian Studies* 65(2): 307–337, https://doi.org/10.1017/S0021911806000003.

Gorospe, Vitaliano R. 1992. 'Mount Banahaw: The power mountain from ritualism to spirituality,' *Philippine Studies* 40(2): 204–218.

Greenblatt, Stephen. 1991. *Marvellous Possessions*. Chicago: University of Chicago Press.

Habkirk, Scott and Hsun Chang. 2017. 'Scents, community, and incense in traditional Chinese religion,' *Material Religion* 13(2): 156–174, https://doi.org/10.1080/17432200.2017.1289306.

Jackson, Peter. 1999. 'The enchanting spirit of Thai capitalism: The cult of Luang Phor Khoon and the post-modernization of Thai Buddhism,' *South East Asian Research* 7(1): 5–60, https://doi.org/10.1177/0967828X9900700102

Jones, Timothy G. 2005. *The Chinese in the Northern Territory*. Darwin: Charles Darwin University Press.

Kuhn, Philip A. 2008. *Chinese Among Others: Emigration in Modern Times*. Lanham, MD: Rowman and Littlefield.

Lakos, William. 2010. *Chinese Ancestor Worship: A Practice and Ritual Oriented Approach to Understanding Chinese Culture*. Cambridge: Cambridge Scholars Publishing.

Latour, Bruno. 2007. *Reassembling the Social: An Introduction to Actor Network Theory*. Oxford: Oxford University Press.

Liu, Tik-sang. 2003. 'A nameless but active religion: An anthropologist's view of local religion in Hong Kong and Macau,' in Daniel L. Overmyer (ed.), *Religion in China Today*, pp. 67–88, *The China Quarterly*, Special Issue 3. Cambridge: Cambridge University Press.

Liu, Zhiwei. 1995. 'Lineage on the sands: The case of Shawan,' in David Faure and Helen F. Siu (eds.), *Down to Earth: The Territorial Bond in South China*, pp. 21–43. Stanford: Stanford University Press.

Mandal, Sumit K. 2012. 'Popular sites of prayer, transoceanic migration, and cultural diversity: Exploring the significance of keramat in Southeast Asia,' *Modern Asian Studies* 46(2): 355–372, https://doi.org/10.1017/S0026749X12000029.

McKeown, Adam. 2001. *Chinese Migrant Networks and Cultural Change: Peru, Chicago, Hawaii, 1900–1936*. Chicago: University of Chicago Press.

Moore, Henrietta L. and Todd Sanders (eds.). 2001. *Magical Interpretations, Material Realities: Modernity, Witchcraft and the Occult in Post-colonial Africa*. London: Routledge.

Munier, Christophe. 1998. *Sacred Rocks and Buddhist Caves in Thailand*. Bangkok: White Lotus Press.

Naquin, Susan and Chun-fang Yu. 1992. 'Introduction,' in Susan Naquin and Chun-Fang Yu (eds.), *Pilgrims and Sacred Sites in China*, pp. 1–38. Berkeley: University of California Press.

Newell, William H. 1962. *Treacherous River: A Study of Rural Chinese in North Malaya*. Kuala Lumpur: University of Malaya Press.

Pena, Elaine, A. 2011. *Performing Piety: Making Space Sacred with the Virgin of Guadalupe*. Berkeley: University of California Press.

Ramsay, Guy. 2003. 'Cherbourg's Chinatown: Creating an identity of place on an Australian Aboriginal settlement,' *Journal of Historical Geography* 29(1): 109–122, https://doi.org/10.1006/jhge.2002.0447.

Rawson, Jessica. 1996. 'Changes in the representation of life and the afterlife as illustrated by the contents of tombs of the T'ang and Sung periods,' in M. Hearn and J. Smith (eds.), *Arts of the Sung and Yuan*, pp. 23–43. New York: Metropolitan Museum of Art.

Rocha, Cristina. 2020. 'Materiality and global spiritual networks: Old and new sacred places and objects,' *Australian Journal of Anthropology* 31: 210–223, https://doi.org/10.1111/taja.12357.

Rocha, Cristina and Manuel A. Vásquez (eds.). 2013. *The Diaspora of Brazilian Religions*. Leiden: Brill.

See, Chinben. 1981. 'Chinese clanship in the Philippine setting,' *Journal of Southeast Asian Studies* 12(1): 224–247, https://doi.org/10.1017/S0022463400005099.

Siu, Helen F. 2016. *Tracing China: A Forty-Year Ethnographic Journey.* Hong Kong: Hong Kong University Press.

Taylor, Charles. 2007. *A Secular Age*. Cambridge, MA: Harvard University Press.

Waitt, Gordon. 2003. 'A place for Buddha in Wollongong, New South Wales? Territorial rules in the place-making of sacred spaces,' *Australian Geographer* 34(2): 223–238, https://doi.org/10.1080/00049180301733.

Watson, James L. 1977. 'Chinese emigrant ties to the home community,' *New Community* 5(4): 343–352, https://doi.org/10.1080/1369183X.1977.9975473.

Widodo, Johannes. 2016. 'Morphogenesis and hybridity in Southeast Asian coastal cities,' in Rahil Esmail, Brian Shaw and Ooi Giok Ling (eds.), *Southeast Asian Culture and Heritage in a Globalising World: Diverging Identities in a Dynamic Region*, pp. 79–92. London: Routledge.

Wong, Dorothy C. 2004. *Chinese Steles: Pre-Buddhist and Buddhist Use of a Symbolic Form*. Honolulu: University of Hawaii Press.

Yang, Mayfair. 2004. 'Spatial struggles: Postcolonial complex, state disenchantment, and popular reappropriation of space in rural south-east China,' *Journal of Asian Studies* 63(3): 719–755, https://doi.org/10.1017/S002191180400169X.

Yang, Mayfair. 2008. 'Goddess across the Taiwan Strait: Matrifocal ritual space, nation-state, and satellite television footprints,' in Mayfair Yang (ed.), *Chinese Religiosities: Afflictions of Modernity and State Formation*, pp. 323–347. Berkeley: University of California Press.

5   Diasporic modernity

In recent decades, countries with a history of taking in large numbers of migrants have turned to consider how to represent this history, in its material form, in their official heritage record. In doing so, there has been a tendency to hone in on migrant 'difference'. By this, I mean a tendency to seek out buildings and places created by migrants that stand out materially from those of the host culture. In Australia, examples include Greek Orthodox churches, Chinese temples, and mosques, all of which are likely to attract heritage attention, especially when they reflect traditional design principles. Also displaying this kind of difference are those Lebanese migrants' houses that feature brick archways and distinctive tilework. The 1950s Greek cafés, which in their interior design brought the aesthetic of coffee culture to tea-drinking Australia, are another example. This is not to say that buildings belonging to the host country's architectural milieu are never classified as migrant heritage – examples include the migrant quarantine stations on Angel Island (San Francisco) and in Sydney.[1] Rather, it points to a noticeable habit of identifying migrant material culture in the destination country on the basis of its reproduction of the traditional, premodern architectural language of the migrant origin country. What I am proposing is that the heritage apparatus, in its quest for difference, sets up a modern–premodern dualism in accord with which it situates non-Western migrants as premodern transplants in a modern world.

Heritage and alterity

This chapter is concerned with the relationship between migrancy and modernity. It will argue that in settler nations, heritage practice's quest for difference, whether consciously or not, taps into that aspect of coloniality that casts the non-Western migrant as the 'other', in this case, the premodern other, the other of white settler culture's supposed forward-looking modernity. At play here is the discursive phenomenon of 'alterity', in terms

DOI: 10.4324/9781003088714-6

of which an identity is constructed in contrast to another entity. Formulated by the philosopher Emmanuel Lévinas, the concept of alterity was taken up in the field of postcolonial studies to describe the manner in which the non-West came to be posited as the West's cultural other. The West's self-identification as modern, progressive and freedom loving came into view, for instance, via a long tradition of depicting the Orient as archaic, unchanging and despotic. Orientalist discourse cast the peoples of the East as 'degraded remnants of former greatness' (Said 1995: 233) – their 'great moments were in the past' (Said 1995: 35). The power and utility of alterity stems, in particular, from the way it has allowed the West to formulate its own racial identity while simultaneously providing a moral underpinning for its subjugation of the 'other world'.

The development of the idea of heritage in the West during the 19th and 20th centuries was steeped in alterity, coinciding as it did with the apogee of West's colonial era and with the popularisation of social evolutionist theory originating in the works of James Frazer, John Lubbock and Henry Lewis Morgan, published between the 1870s and 1890s. The conception of the cultures of Asia as antique was accompanied by the idea that the West had a responsibility, as the more evolved civilisation, to exercise custodianship of the ancient monuments of the East. Of more immediate relevance to this chapter, however, is the question of what happens when the East, in the form of migrants from China, takes up residence in the West. What is seen in Australia, as noted earlier, has been a tendency for heritage practitioners over the last half-century to construct a category of 'migrant heritage' that, in focusing on material difference (e.g., the Chinese temple), has in a sense locked Chinese migrant culture into the same category of the 'antique' that the West projected onto China in earlier centuries. In the following section, I will show how this projection was at odds with the modern subjectivity of Chinese migrants themselves. But first, it is worth considering for a moment the question of how alterity may operate at an invisible level in heritage practice.

Heritage practitioners may feel it *necessary* to highlight what they see as the ethnic-cultural distinctiveness of buildings associated with migrants, working from the assumption that otherwise the public at large will simply not recognise them as the heritage of a particular migrant group. In this way, the traditional upturned eaves of the green ceramic-tiled roof of a Chinese temple erected by migrants in a place like Sydney comes to be employed as an ethnic marker in heritage practice. The distinctiveness of the temple roof counters a lack of distinction elsewhere, in this case, a lack arising from the fact that Chinese migrants in the late 1800s and early 1900s overwhelming utilised existing Anglo-Australian building stock to accommodate themselves and their businesses. And where they did build for themselves, they overwhelmingly chose the architectural styles fashionable in the country at the time. And yet, ironically, by engaging in the discourse of 'difference', heritage practice actually works to assimilate migrants into the host society, assigning them a place in it by the mechanism of creating a category for their 'places' (temples, mosques, cafés and so on) in the host's heritage inventory. In other words, by finding a place for them in the national narrative, it strives to *settle* them, just as, by invoking a one-way, linear narrative of migrant life that has no space for transnational connectivity, it confines the material past of the migrant experience within the nation's territorial boundaries (Byrne 2016). The alternative to an alterity-based heritage approach would be one that, for example, relied not on buildings 'speaking their own name' through their architectural style but on interpreting their social history and on interrogating the material traces – often easily missed – of the ways migrants adapted the buildings to their lifestyle and their lifestyle to the buildings. Far from being technically ambitious, such an approach would be well within the present capability of those working in the fields of public history, heritage studies and historical archaeology.

Chinese migrants as modern subjects

In Australia, it was indigenous people and Chinese migrants who, characterised as primitive and unchanging others, brought into view the supposed modernity of 'white Australia' (Anderson 2005: 331; Fitzgerald 2007). From the 1890s through the early decades of the 20th century, Chinese migrants in Australia, by performing a modern subjectivity, countered this construction of themselves. They were, according to John Fitzgerald,

> among the first Australians to embrace modern technologies and take up modishly modern lifestyles. In the 1890s they rode the latest bicycles, in the 1900s they wore sober business suits and flounced dresses, in the 1910s they picnicked by the seaside, in the 1920s they ran radio repair shops and in wartime they flew Australian flags. Chinese Australians probably travelled more frequently than whites and they discovered in their travels that Australia was one of the very few countries where all of the technological and ethical promises of modernity were on offer.
>
> (Fitzgerald 2007: 29)

Many of them, in what Shirley Lim (2012: 162) describes as an enactment of 'cultural citizenship', played tennis, attended debutante balls and had their photos taken in front of the late-model cars and trucks they owned.

Here we have a lifestyle and material culture that on the face of it appears radically at odds with the Orientalist construction of Chinese migrants as representatives of a premodern culture incapable of change. What complicates this picture is that this lifestyle also included elements of 'traditional' Chinese culture, such as the practice of ancestor worship that was an accompaniment of lineage membership, consumption of Chinese herbal medicines and the incorporation of Confucian ethics in business practices. As Adam McKeown (2001: 280) observes in relation to Chinese Americans in the same period, their embrace of modernity 'was not a transformative disjuncture but a complex array of shifts and partial shifts.' What occurred was not a straightforward adoption of modern Western norms and products, mixing them with discrete elements of traditional Chinese practices and products. Rather, what is seen is the emergence of an alternative modernity that reworked elements of both Western modernity and Chinese traditional culture to produce something quite original. We must also keep in mind how deeply Eurocentric and historically inaccurate the notion of a changeless China always was. Until the advent of European industrialisation in the 18th century, China was a leading global force in scientific and technological invention (Pomeranz 2000) and through the very period of emigration from southern China that is the focus of much of this book, the country was undergoing immense political and cultural change and was swirling with new ideas, as exemplified in the May Fourth Movement (Schwarcz 1990), and new products (some of which are described in Chapter 3).

The self-conscious modernity of many Chinese–Australians, which they had in common with their counterparts in North America, carried over into the modernising projects, discussed earlier in the book, which they carried out in their home counties in China. These projects included the building of railways and electricity plants (Hsu 2000: 48–49). It certainly informed the style of the houses that migrants from Zhongshan built in their ancestral villages (Chapter 3), although we need to be careful to distinguish between modernity and modernist architecture (Chang and Lim 2012: 17). These houses, some in a modified-traditional form and others in local renditions of European neoclassical style, represented the spirit of modernity in architecture.[2] They were, however, anything but *modernist*, either in terms of Bauhaus principles or by affinity to the actual modernist buildings appearing in Chinese cities such as Shanghai and Canton in the 1920s and 1930s (Rowe and Kuan 2002). The Zhongshan houses were modern by virtue of having departed, by about the 1910s, from the architecture of the vernacular house. Those who commissioned and built the houses had access to a panoply of 'new' architectural styles – most notably neoclassicism – favoured by the Chinese and Western elites present in Zhongshan's neighbouring cities, which in order of proximity were Macao, Hong Kong and Canton (now Guangzhou).

There is no evidence that Zhongshan migrants in Australia channelled new housing styles or building technologies back to their villages in China (these came from closer at hand, particularly from Hong Kong). Rather, what they channelled back was a modern frame of mind, which itself was a product not of Australia but of a broader sphere of experience.[3] Many of them were participants in a transnational culture of modernity that spanned the 'Cantonese Pacific' (Yu 2011). And all of them, in one way or another, were participants in the emergent modern culture of the Pearl River Delta. Participating in that emergent culture were those who returned to Zhongshan to visit, often for extended periods, and those who returned permanently but chose to base themselves in Hong Kong while still maintaining links with their village (Williams 2018: 26, 48–49). For those remaining in Australia, their participation was primarily via remittances, letters, and by being networked to modern China via Chinese language newspapers and through their involvement in such institutions of 'diaspora nationalism' as the Kuomintang (Kuo 2013: 158–159).

Confident that an immense appetite for modern life existed in China, a number of Chinese migrant entrepreneurs in Sydney were motivated to open the first department stores in Hong Kong, Guangzhou and Shanghai, beginning in 1910. The Sincere company founded by the Ma brothers and the Wing On company by the Gock brothers were capitalised partly from small investments made by Chinese store owners and market garden operators in rural and urban New South Wales (with other investors from among the Chinese business communities of the USA and Hawaii). The success of the Sincere and Wing On stores in Hong Kong and the Chinese mainland was underwritten by modern retailing principles: fixed prices, quality guarantee, uniformed staff, print media advertising and glamorous window displays modelled by their founders on Sydney's Anthony Hordern department store that was situated close to the city's Chinatown (Chan 1996; Fitzgerald 2007: 191–199). The department stores recruited staff from among the founders' extended families and clans, and among those who simply shared 'native place' (*qiaoxiang*) ties to Zhongshan and thus spoke the Zhongshan dialect of Cantonese. This included Zhongshanese living in Australia.

The department store buildings erected by these entrepreneurs in neoclassical and then later in 'international style' were the acme of modernity, featuring elevators and including among their merchandise the latest clothing fashions, wristwatches, fountain pens and modern appliances. Today, a whole floor of the Museum of Commercial Culture in Zhongshan is devoted to the history of the Sincere and Wing On department store empires. On display are superbly rendered one-metre-high scale models of the store buildings and a full-scale diorama of the shoe department of one of the stores where a mannequin of a young woman with a 1920s hairstyle and contemporary cheongsam is shown trying on a pair of shoes while her companion, a young man in a silver mohair suit, watches on (Figure 5.1). Though they were located beyond Zhongshan, the department stores are considered part of its legacy on the grounds that founders of the stores were native to Zhongshan. Meanwhile, in Shanghai, the elaborate six-storey Sincere and Wing On stores, built in the 1910s and standing opposite each other at an intersection on Nanjing Road, have been absorbed into the city's heritage

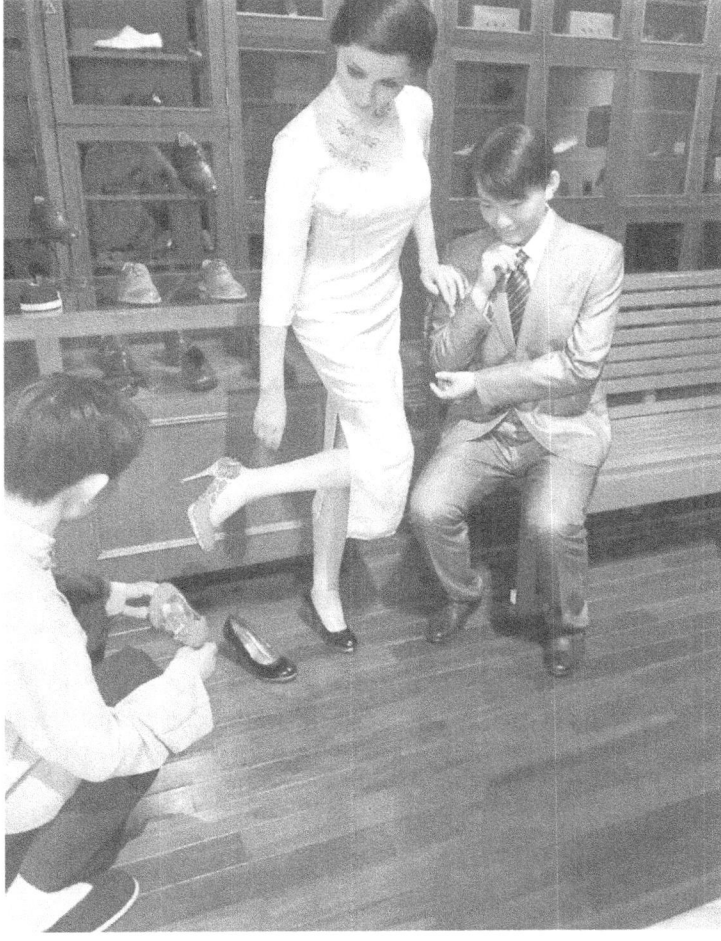

Figure 5.1 Diorama of the shoe department in a department store built in China in the early 20th century by returned migrants from Australia, Museum of Commercial Culture, Zhongshan.

inventory. Some of the Zhongshan migrants and migrant descendants inter-viewed in Sydney during research for this book count the department stores as elements of their personal heritage.[4] The department stores, in material and storied form, continue to resonate at both ends of the China–Australia migration corridor.

Chinatown: an Orientalist representation of Chineseness

Chinese urban enclaves emerged during the 19th century in cities as diverse as San Francisco, Honolulu, Lima and Sydney (Anderson 1990, 1991; Anderson et al. 2019; McKeown 2001). Though each was a response to particular social-political conditions in the host country, broadly speaking each was also a response to the desire to have a home away from home, a place of relative security in a larger environment that was hostile, to varying degrees, to the Chinese as a 'race'. Characteristic of each of these enclaves was an almost complete absence of a distinctive Chinese architecture. What made them distinctively 'Chinese' to non-Chinese residents of the cities was the abundant signage in Chinese characters, the goods from China displayed in shop windows, the exotic aromas wafting from restaurants, and the sight of people wearing traditional clothing and, in the case of men, hair braided in a queue.[5] None of these, however, left a lasting impression in the urban fabric of the kind that would translate as material heritage.

Then, on 18 April 1906, the Great San Francisco earthquake, the ensuing fire, and the demolition of buildings to create firebreaks destroyed that city's Chinatown. The old Chinatown had consisted of Victorian commercial brick buildings, distinguished from others of their kind in the city only by the large porcelain flowerpots on their wooden balconies and the silk Chinese lanterns hanging from the balcony roofs. Even the temple built in 1869 was in Victorian style, only the Chinese charters on a marble plaque identifying it as Chinese (Choy 2008: 8). But immediately after the quake, leading Chinese merchants and community leaders began planning an 'Oriental City' in the space of the old Chinatown, aiming to attract non-Chinese tourists by playing on their appetite for exoticism (Choy 2012: 43). Local non-Chinese architects developed a new 'Sino-architectural vocabulary' that included pseudo-traditional tiled roofs with upturned eaves, to lend a veneer of Chineseness to what underneath were conventional 'American' structures of reinforced concrete and brick (Choy 2012: 45). The strategy proved remarkably effective during the following decades in making Chinatown a tourism destination. In Vancouver in 1936, on the occasion of the city's Golden Jubilee celebrations, Chinese merchants and leaders funded a similar makeover of the Chinese migrant enclave as a tourist attraction, erecting a giant bamboo archway, a nine-tier pagoda and other features to guarantee, in the eyes of its creators, a '100 percent Celestial atmosphere' (Anderson 1991: 196). As in San Francisco, both the city administration and the white public thoroughly approved.

How are we to explain how this attraction to the Oriental on the part of non-Chinese Americans and Canadians was able to exist concurrently with an aversion to Chinese persons? San Francisco's new Chinatown began emerging at a time when, a quarter of a century after the 1882 Chinese Exclusion Act had prevented Chinese Americans becoming US citizens, anti-Chinese immigration laws and regulations were being implemented, measures reflecting a widespread popular hostility to Chinese–Americans (McKeown 2008). The co-occurrence of attraction and aversion, or what in this specific case has been called 'desire and difference' (Lee 2001: 7), seems to lie in the nature of Orientalism, that aestheticised structure for understanding the Orient, referred to earlier, which developed in Europe in the late 18th century. Orientalism, in Edward Said's classic formulation, is:

> ...the corporate institution for dealing with the Orient, dealing with it by making statements about it, authorizing views of it, describing it, by teaching it, settling it, ruling over it: in short, Orientalism as a Western style for dominating, restructuring, and having authority over the Orient.' The Orientalising gaze has always abstracted the material culture of the East away from the people who produced and used it.
>
> (Said 1995: 3)

It was and is entirely possible for people of the West to admire the classical art and architecture of China – even in the gimcrack way it is represented in Chinatowns – without admiring or even admitting racial equality with the Chinese people inhabiting the landscape it stands in. As with the classical art and architecture of Greece, the West styled itself in cultural evolutionist terms as the legitimate inheritor of ancient Oriental art and architecture over the heads, as it were, of the modern peoples of the Orient. In heritage practice, this continues to be manifest in a custodial attitude to 'protecting' ancient monuments from the indigenous people living amongst them today, something Tim Winter (2006) critiques in relation to Angkorean ruins in Cambodia. It is something I have discussed in regard to conservation efforts by heritage authorities in Taiwan and Thailand that privilege the aesthetic surface of old Chinese temples and Buddhist stupas over practices of popular religion that constantly work to 'update' them by adding new fabric and new renditions of sacred art (Byrne 2014, 2020).

Perhaps the most interesting aspect of the Chinatown phenomenon in San Francisco and Vancouver is that it was the Chinese communities themselves that instigated, or at least collaborated in, this reimagining of their urban enclaves along Orientalist lines. Writing of Vancouver's Chinatown, Kay Anderson (1991) refers to this phenomenon as a strategic borrowing by overseas Chinese of the West's reification of Chineseness in order to achieve their own ends. In this act of 'self-Orientalism' (Anderson et al. 2019: 28), migrant Chinese are seen to have been conscious of Orientalism as a power-saturated discourse capable of being hijacked by subalterns and turned back on the West. As Anderson observes, '[c]ategorizations of identity and place may "act back" across time, as those historically subject to classification begin to project that ascription in the political arena in order to realize interests of their own' (1991: 179). The interests in question lay in countering or ameliorating anti-Chinese racist attitudes. This was to be achieved by diverting white attention away from themselves and towards the mythology of an essentialised premodern Chineseness, allowing them more space to get on with the business of being modern. Which is to say, by diverting white attention to a mythologised past, they could live unmolested in the present.

'Core culture' and 'core heritage'

The advent of multiculturalist policies in Australia and Canada in the 1970s saw a turn on the part of governments and a large part of the white public from constructions of Chineseness based on biological essentialism to an idea of ethnic difference that was culturally based (Anderson 1991: 217). Urban planners in each of these cities now saw the potential of Chinatown to become a metaphor for multicultural inclusiveness. In Vancouver, new streetscaping of the city's Chinatown included the planting of trees from China, the installation of Hong Kong-style bilingual street signs and of street lighting in the form of 'Chinese' lanterns (Anderson 1991: 228). In Sydney, garbage bins with 'Chinese' motifs and lantern-style streetlights were installed, and pseudo-traditional green-tiled portico roofs tacked onto the façade of restaurants and shops (Anderson et al. 2019: 26). In both places, after some persuasion by urban planners, Chinese merchants and community leaders lent their support to what were essentially Orientalising projects originating within multiculturalist discourse. The production of Chinatown, as Anderson (1990, 1991) shows, has always been grounded in an obsession with 'difference': racial difference in the first half of the 20th century, ethnic-cultural difference in the second.

This is not meant to diminish the distinction between multiculturalism and the blatantly racist immigration policies of the first half of the 20th century. There obviously is a weighty distinction between policies that exclude and discriminate on racial grounds and policies that take a celebratory approach to ethnic difference. Rather, my intention is to point to the way alterity can persist through time in different guises. It has been argued in the case of Australia, for example, that there exists a discursively entrenched and hegemonic perception among many white Australians that the country has a 'core' culture that is Anglo, and that while a diversity of new immigrant cultures may be a good thing for the country, the core remains intact (Forrest and Dunn 2006). Ghassan Hage (1998) maintains that embedded in multiculturalism is the idea that while non-Anglo migrants enrich Australia's culture, they cannot fundamentally change it. The notion of cultural intactness on display here has its counterpart in that strain of heritage practice that privileges the original fabric of old buildings over later accretions and modifications, leading to the practice of 'restoring' such buildings back to a semblance of their original material state. This is to indulge in the myth that it is possible to take a building back in time, a myth sustained by erasing all trace of the changes a building accumulates through its history of occupation and use. The end product of restoration can, of course, only ever be some semblance or simulacrum of the original, since even the act of restoration inevitably adds to the original fabric – for example, by the application of chemical stabilising agents, by the insertion of 'damp courses' in walls or by repointing brick or stone walls with new mortar. Restoration is thus always additive as much as it is subtractive (of accretions) and is best thought of as a building practice in its own right (Byrne 2020: 867). One further point to be made is that the events of a building's post-construction life will also almost always leave scars on its body, in the form for instance of nail and screw holes in walls and use-wear on floorboards and wooden stairs that are virtually impossible to remove during restoration. They can only be erased by 'taking back' the surfaces of walls and floors, leading to a physical diminishment of the original.

Put in the context of the materiality of migration, it seems clear that the notion of the recoverable original in heritage practice invokes something rather similar to the idea of an ineradicable core culture – each invokes an entity whose essence is held to be unaltered and unalloyed by its passage through time and its encounters with others. What I am suggesting is that the notion of core culture has its counterpart in that of what I would call 'core heritage'. I want now to pick up again the thread of the discussion in the first section of this chapter on the tendency of Chinese migrants to have utilised existing Anglo-Australian building stock rather than building houses and business premises for themselves, in whatever style suited them. What, it may be asked, are the implications of this in relation to the concept of 'core heritage'? In conventional heritage practice and under the hegemony of 'core heritage', the Anglo-Australian building stock used by Chinese migrants retains its identity as Anglo-Australian regardless of the intensity or longevity of occupation by Chinese migrants who rented or purchased the buildings in question. The identity of the buildings is taken to be determined and fixed by the macro level of their architectural style rather than the micro level of the kind of markings of occupant use discussed earlier, which might also be described as a sedimentation of lives lived in the buildings. In heritage discourse, the identity of the buildings is, as it were, stamped on them at birth. The result is that Chinese migrant histories become largely illegible in the heritage landscape. Anglo-Australian culture retains its dominance there.

Bringing the discussion back to the theme of modernity and the ways in which Chinese migrant heritage in the West has been characterised as an expression of premodernity, I would make the point that although Anglo-Australian culture is construed by many white Australians as immune to modification by interaction with other migrant cultures, it is not by any means seen by them to be static. On the contrary, progressiveness is held to be key element of the white identity. Relevant here is the fact that Progressivism was a powerful political force in Australian politics between the 1880s and 1920s (as it was in the USA). Grounded in the ideal of creating a society that was new and 'better' than the old societies of Europe (Lake 2019), the Progressives pushed through democratic reforms to the electoral system, including women's suffrage, but equally they were virulently racist in their attitudes to and policies aimed at Asian migrants and indigenous Australians.

The progressivist ambition of building a new society and nation (for the white race) is not unrelated, I suggest, to the building of Australia in the material sense. While the faux-traditional green-tiled portico roofs and lantern-style street lights of Chinatown have been used as a marker of an unchanging 'Chineseness', white Australia has found its identity partly in ambitious building projects such as the Sydney Harbour Bridge, erected in 1923–1932, and in the Sydney Opera House built between 1959 and 1973, both ranked at the country's highest level of heritage classification.[6] They have been taken as epitomising Australia's modernity and progressiveness, casting White Australia as a nation of builders. In the logic of alterity, Chinese Australians were implicitly construed as non-builders, at least in the sense of not being creators of a progressive infrastructure and architecture. At best, as in the case of the temples they built in Australia, they have been cast as *replicators*, reproducers of an architecture that, however admirable it might be, is antique and timeless.

The Snowy Mountains hydropower project (1949–1974) warrants mention here. Seventy percent of the 100,000 people employed on the project were migrants arriving in Australia from the late 1940s from a Europe devastated by World War II.[7] The Australian Government's statement of significance for the 2016 listing of the project on the National Heritage List describes it as 'an enduring symbol of Australia's identity as a multicultural, independent, and resourceful country.'[8] Whereas the numerous irrigation and hydropower dams constructed in Spain from the 1940s to the 1970s were exploited for their propaganda value in extolling the technological progressiveness of Franco's fascist regime – they constituted Franco's hydro-social 'wet dream' (Swyngedouw 2007) – in Australia, the Snowy Mountains project became, at least retrospectively, a monument to multiculturalism. What the Australian government's statement of significance for the project neglects to mention, however, is that the White Australia policy was not significantly dismantled until 1966 – up until then, the cultural inclusiveness celebrated by the listing was shadowed by explicit policies to exclude of non-Europeans from the country's immigration program. This ensured that the building of what remains the largest public works engineering scheme ever undertaken in Australia would be a white enterprise.

Concrete modernity

As a counter to the image of Chinese immigrants as premodern, I conclude this chapter with a very brief consideration of their involvement with that most quintessential of building materials, reinforced concrete. The advent of the technology of reinforced concrete in Europe and America in the first half of the 20th century had a major impact on architecture in the non-Western world (for Asia, see Chua 2019; Denison and Ren 2008; Mahatmanto 2018). In the main migrant-sending provinces of China, Fujian and Guangdong, the diaspora was closely involved in the adoption of the technology, particularly in building houses for themselves and their relatives in their ancestral villages. While there was little to associate Chinese immigrants in Australia in the pre-1940s period with architectural modernity, back in the home villages of Zhongshan they were at its cutting edge.

Although widely employed in the Roman empire, concrete subsequently fell out of use as a building material in Europe, only to emerge again with the invention of Portland cement in England in 1824 and the development from the 1850s of steel-reinforced concrete simultaneously in France, Germany and England (Forty 2012: 30–32). In East Asia, Japan in 1871 began producing its own Portland cement, an essential ingredient of modern concrete, as part of the Meiji Revolution's program of rapid modernisation (Nishizawa 2014). The first Portland cement factory in the area of South China was established in 1886 on Green Island, off Macau (immediately to the south of Zhongshan County), by a British company, and in 1907 the Chinese government built one in Canton (Clements 1922). Reinforced concrete was being used in buildings in Hong Kong by the 1910s and by the

1920s in Zhongshan County, 70 kilometres away on the Chinese mainland, many of the remittance houses of Chinese Australians incorporated reinforced concrete columns, roof beams and floor plates. In Kaiping County, 60 kilometres southwest of Zhongshan, most of the tower houses (*diaolou*) built by diaspora Chinese between the 1910s and the 1930s (Figure 3.8) had reinforced concrete frames (Batto 2006).

Whereas, in Australia, Chinese immigrants were cast as representatives of a premodern, timeless Asia, in China they were seen by their fellow villages as the acme of innovation and modernity. Their concrete-framed houses, rising proudly above the roofs of those villagers who lacked overseas connections, testified to this, as did the very mobility of the migrants. Travel, and mobility more generally, have long been considered key elements of modernity. 'Mobility', in Tim Cresswell's words, has been 'central to the constitution of the modern' (Cresswell 2006: 18). Given the transnational travel entailed in their migration, Chinese migrants in America, Australia, Europe and elsewhere might almost be said to have been modern by virtue of simply being there. Oceanic travel indeed became a status symbol in the emigrant villages of the Pearl River Delta, and the ocean liners depicted in wall paintings in many of the houses built by overseas Chinese in those villages (Figure 5.2) were statements of their owners' belonging to the modern world.

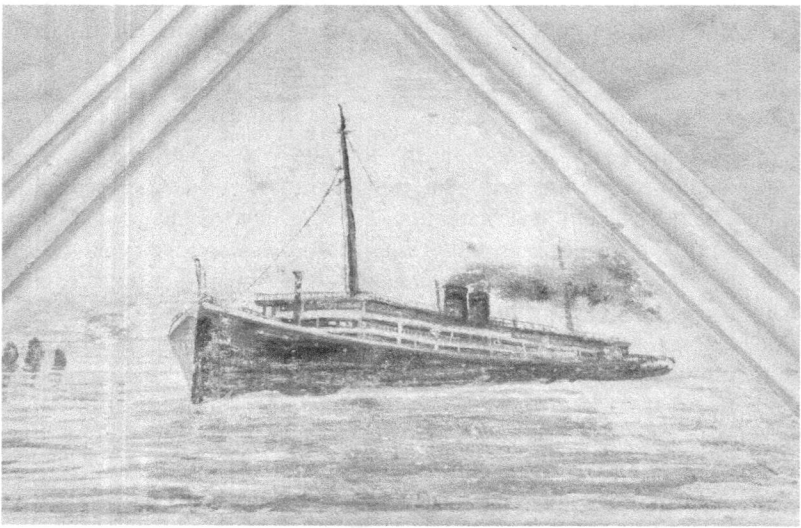

Figure 5.2 A painting of an ocean liner on the exterior of a remittance house (c.1920s) in Buck Toy village, Zhongshan.

Notes

1 For the Sydney quarantine station, see www.qstation.com.au/our-story.html; for the Angel Island quarantine station, see https://angelisland.org/history/quaran tine-station/
2 Neville Morley (2009) has argued that modernity in Europe was steeped in the classical past and framed by reference to that past.
3 This is not to say that migrants elsewhere and at other times have not imported architectural styles from their destination countries back into their home villages in the course of constructing remittance houses. Lopez (2015: 64–65) describes the occurrence of this in remittance houses in Guanajuato, Mexico.
4 See, for example, Denise Ma, a descendant of the founders of the Sincere Company www.heritagecorridor.org.au/people/denise-ma
5 While Europeans in the destination countries took the queue to be a marker of Chineseness, actually the hairstyle had been imposed on Han Chinese by the Manchu after they invaded China in 1636. It was loathed by many Chinese as a symbol of oppression.
6 For National Heritage List details for the Sydney Harbour Bridge, see www. environment.gov.au/heritage/places/national/sydney-harbour-bridge. For National Heritage List details for the Sydney Opera House, see www.environment.gov.au/ heritage/places/national/sydney-opera-house
7 See National Heritage listing statement: www.environment.gov.au/heritage/ places/national/snowy-mountains-scheme
8 See www.environment.gov.au/heritage/places/national/snowy-mountains-scheme

References

Anderson, Kay. 1990. ' "Chinatown re-oriented": A critical analysis of recent rede-velopment schemes in a Melbourne and Sydney enclave,' *Australian Geographical Studies* 18(2): 137–154, https://doi.org/10.1111/j.1467-8470.1990.tb00609.x.
Anderson, Kay. 1991. *Vancouver's Chinatown: Racial Discourse in Canada, 1875–1980*. Montreal: McGill-Queen's University Press.
Anderson, Kay, Ien Ang, Andrea Del Bono, Donald McNeill and Alexandra Wong. 2019. *Chinatown Unbound: Trans-Asian Urbanism in the Age of China*. London: Rowman and Littlefield.
Anderson, Kay and Affrica Taylor. 2005. 'Exclusionary politics and the question of national belonging: Australian ethnicities in "multiscalar" focus,' *Ethnicities* 5: 460–485, https://doi.org/10.1177/1468796805058095.
Batto, Patricia R. S. 2006. 'The diaolou of Kaiping (1842–1937): Building for dangerous times,' *China Perspectives* 66: 2–18, https://doi.org/10.4000/chinaperspec tives.1033.
Byrne, Denis. 2014. *Counterheritage: Critical Perspectives on Heritage Conservation in Asia*. New York: Routledge.
Byrne, Denis. 2016. 'Heritage corridors: Transnational flows and the built environment of migration,' *Journal of Ethnic and Migration Studies* 42(14): 2351–2369, https://doi.org/10.1080/1369183X.2016.1205805.
Byrne, Denis. 2020. 'Divinely significant: Towards a postsecular approach to the materiality of popular religion in Asia,' *International Journal of Heritage Studies* 26(9): 857–873, https://doi.org/10.1080/13527258.2019.1590447.

Chan, Wellington K. K. 1996. 'Organization and strategy of China's two premier department stores: The Wing On and Sincere companies, 1900–1941,' in Leo Douw and Peter Post (eds.), *South China: State, Culture and Social Change During the 20th Century*, pp. 183–193. Amsterdam: Royal Netherlands Academy of Arts and Sciences; New York: Oxford University Press.

Chang, Jiat-Hwee and William S. W. Lim. 2012. 'Non west modernist past: Rethinking modernisms and modernities beyond the west,' in William S. W. Lim and Jiat-Hwee Chang (eds.), *Non West Modernist Past: On Architecture and Modernities*, pp. 7–24. Singapore: World Scientific Publishing.

Choy, Philip P. 2008. *The Architecture of San Francisco Chinatown*. San Francisco: Chinese Historical Society of America.

Choy, Philip P. 2012. *San Francisco Chinatown: A Guide to Its History and Architecture*. San Francisco: City Lights.

Chua, Lawrence. 2019. 'The aesthetic citizen: Translating modernism and fascism in mid-twentieth-century Thailand,' in William S. W. Lim and Jiat-Hwee Chang (eds.), *Non West Modernist Past: On Architecture and Modernities*, pp. 58–84. Singapore: World Scientific Publishing.

Clements, Morgan. 1922. 'The cement industry of China,' *Millards Weekly Review* 20(12): 454–458.

Cresswell, Tim. 2006. *On the Move: Mobility in the Modern Western World*. London: Routledge.

Denison, Edward and Guang Yu Ren. 2008. *Modernism in China: Architectural Visions and Revolutions*. London: Wiley.

Fitzgerald, John. 2007. *Big White Lie: Chinese Australians in White Australia*. Sydney: University of New South Wales Press.

Forrest, James and Kevin Dunn. 2006. ' "Core" culture hegemony and multiculturalism: Perceptions of the privileged position of Australians with British backgrounds,' *Ethnicities* 6(2): 203–230.

Forty, Adrian. 2012. *Concrete and Culture: A Material History*. London: Reaktion.

Hage, Ghassan. 1998. *White Nation: Fantasies of White Supremacy in a Multicultural Society*. Sydney: Pluto.

Hsu, Madeline Y. 2000. *Dreaming of Gold, Dreaming of Home: Transnationalism and Migration Between the United States and South China 1882–1943*. Stanford: Stanford University Press.

Kuo, Mei-fen. 2013. *Making Chinese Australia: Urban Elites, Newspapers and the Formation of Chinese-Australian Identity, 1892–1912*. Melbourne: Monash University Publishing.

Lake, Marilyn. 2019. *Progressive New World: How Settler Colonialism and Transpacific Exchange Shaped American Reform*. Cambridge, MA: Harvard University Press.

Lee, Anthony W. 2001. *Picturing Chinatown: Art and Orientalism in San Francisco*. Berkeley: University of California Press.

Lim, Shirley Jennifer. 2012. 'Glamorising racial modernity,' in David Walker and Agnieszka Sobocinska (eds.), *Australia's Asia: From Yellow Peril to Asian Century*, pp. 145–169. Perth: University of Western Australia Publishing.

Lopez, Sarah Lynn. 2015. *The Remittance Landscape: Spaces of Migration in Rural Mexico and Urban USA*. Chicago: University of Chicago Press.

Mahatmanto. 2018. 'Role of the Journal of Building Engineers in the Dutch East Indies in discussing the emergence of Indonesian modern architecture,' *Journal of Asian Architecture and Building Engineering* 14(3): 529–532, https://doi.org/10.3130/jaabe.14.529.

McKeown, Adam M. 2008. *Melancholy Order: Asian Migration and the Globalization of Borders*. New York: Columbia University Press.

McKeown, Adam, M. 2001. *Chinese Migrant Networks and Cultural Change: Peru, Chicago, and Hawaii, 1900–1936*. Chicago: University of Chicago Press.

Morley, Neville. 2009. *Antiquity and Modernity*. Chichester, UK: Wiley-Blackwell.

Nishizawa, Yasukiho. 2014. 'A study of Japanese colonial architecture in East Asia,' in Izumi Kuroishi (ed.), *Constructing the Colonized Land: Entwined Perspectives of East Asia around WWII*, pp. 11–41. Farnham, UK: Ashgate.

Pomeranz, Kenneth. 2000. *The Great Difference: China, Europe and the Making of the Modern World Economy*. Princeton, NJ: Princeton University Press.

Rowe, Peter G. and Seng Kuan. 2002. *Architectural Encounters with Essence and Form in Modern China*. Cambridge, MA: MIT Press.

Said, Edward W. 1995. *Orientalism: Western Conceptions of the Orient*. London: Penguin.

Schwarcz, Vera. 1990. *The Chinese Enlightenment: Intellectuals and the Legacy of the May Fourth Movement of 1919*. Berkeley: University of California Press.

Swyngedouw, Erik. 2007. 'Technonatural revolutions: The scalar politics of Franco's hydro-social dream for Spain, 1939–1975,' *Transactions of the Institute of British Geographers* 32(1): 9–28, https://doi.org/10.1111/j.1475-5661.2007.00233.x.

Williams, Michael. 2018. *Returning Home with Glory: Chinese Villagers Around the Pacific, 1849 to 1949*. Hong Kong: Hong Kong University Press.

Winter, Tim. 2006. *Expressions of Cambodia: The Politics of Tradition, Identity and Change*. London: Routledge.

Yu, Henry. 2011. 'Intermittent rhythms of the Cantonese Pacific,' in Donna R. Gabaccia and Dirk Hoerder (eds.), *Connecting Seas and Connected Ocean Rims: Indian, Atlantic, and Pacific Oceans and China Seas Migrations from the 1830s to the 1930s*, pp. 393–414. Leiden: Brill.

6   Making heritage in the transnational landscape of migration

Heritage is made rather than found. It takes shape from the imaginative and physical work of people and institutions in the present as they make sense of and give particular meaning to surviving objects from the past that share space with them on the planetary surfaces we inhabit. This is not to say that heritage is not real, it is simply to underline the agency of those people in the present who are engaged in the work of heritage-making. In the case of the heritage of migration, and specifically the heritage of the China–Australia migration corridor, a variety of actors have been at work in this domain, including national and local governments who are able to draw on the resources of heritage bureaucracies and on their legislative and regulatory powers, and individual migrants and their descendants drawing on their memories, inherited collections of letters, documents and photographs and, increasingly, on material sourced from social media and publicly available archives accessible online.

The chapter's first two sections examine the contrasting ways that the heritage of migration has been approached at a state level at either end of the China–Australia migration corridor. In Australia's case, the overarching discursive frame has been that of migrant arrival in and adaptation to life in Australia. It is an inclusionary narrative closely allied to and indeed interwoven with the ideology of multiculturalism. In China, however, the state frames its history and heritage of migration in terms of diaspora loyalty and the contribution of overseas Chinese to the home country's progress. In Australia, the state constructs a 'bordered', nationalist narrative of migration as a one-way journey to a better place, and while China's emphasis on transnational flows might suggest an internationalist perspective, the flows are conceived as occurring within a kind of 'distributed' nation of people who, though globally distributed, are forever essentially Chinese.

In their approach to the heritage of migration, to what extent are heritage experts able to transcend the nation-state 'container' framing of migration heritage? How are they to do justice to the transnational simultaneity (Levitt

DOI: 10.4324/9781003088714-7

and Glick Schiller 2004) that has pervaded the lived experience of migration? One thing to say is that those working in the field of heritage are not helped in this by the weight of the heritage field's own past, by which I mean by the particular way the idea of heritage took form in the emergence of the modern nation-state. The nation-state has finessed an abiding and almost religious conflation of itself with the material past lying within its borders, however ancient that past and however recent the borders (Anderson 1991; Hamilakis 2007; Handler 1988). As Tim Winter (2015: 343) observes, despite the efforts of UNESCO to foster an internationalist approach to heritage conservation, the 'ties that bind archaeology and architectural conservation to formations of nationalism and nation-making, that emerged in various parts of the world from the late nineteenth century onwards, remain as vibrant as ever.' A particular challenge for a heritage practice seeking to transcend the parameters of the nation-state in order to do justice to the cross-border flows and the transnational material world of past and present migration is that the sheer physical solidity and weight of built heritage seem to resist efforts to depict it in territorially fluid terms. Even when created by migrants whose lives are steeped in mobility, this heritage appears rooted in the terrain of distinct nation-states. Buildings have their foundations in the very soil and 'geo-body' (Winichakul 1994) of the nation, while in-ground archaeological traces of migration are buried in that soil. This appearance of being grounded in and contained by the nation makes it too easy for heritage practice to always default to the nation-state as the unit of analysis, something I return to at the end of this chapter. What is called for is a perspective on the buildings associated with migration, be they remittance houses at the sending-country end of a migration corridor or migrant business premises at the migrant-receiving end, that acknowledges their nature as distributed entities, in other words, as assemblages of human and nonhuman actors that are dispersed across nation-state boundaries (Byrne 2016: 275–277).

Migrant heritage in Australia: the one-way narrative frame

From 1945 until the late 1960s, Australian government policy was to assimilate immigrants into an Australian society still defined as ethnically and culturally British. The priority placed on increasing Australia's population meant there was an emphasis on family migration and permanent settlement (Foster and Stockley 1984: 28). Given the one-way, unilinear policy template for immigration, the unanticipated high rates of return migration during this era were a source of embarrassment and worry for Australian governments of the day (Foster and Stockley 1984: 32, 36). For many white Australians, it 'offended national pride' (Lopez 2000: 235).[1] This says a lot about the political environment in which the idea of celebrating migration heritage gained voice; in particular, it speaks to the fact that when the idea took traction in the 1980s, its focus was not on the heritage of migration as such – this would have meant including the material record of sojourning, return migration and transnational placemaking – but on a heritage of immigrant *settlement*. It reflected the government's post-war adherence to an inside–outside binary in which arrival meant permanent settlement and departure meant permanent alienation. This masked the reality that many migrant departures took the form of long visits to the homeland followed by return to Australia, a pattern that had been common among 19th-century Chinese migrants in Australia (Fitzgerald 2007: 53) and is consonant with a flexible, mobile conception of belonging that eludes the category of permanence (see Sheller 2003: 276–277).

By 1994, a total of 112 places had been listed on the Register of the National Estate for their significance to migrant groups, including archaeological remains and built structures representing Chinese presence on the Australian goldfields in the mid-19th century. Although comprising only 1.2 percent of the 8,279 historic places on the register at that point (Purdie 1997: 33), the presence of these 112 sites on the national inventory was significant in reflecting, firstly, a concerted push by a number of historians, archaeologists and heritage experts over the preceding decade or so to document and record sites of non-Anglo migrant activity[2] and, secondly, the advent in Australia between 1973 and 1978 of the ideology of multiculturalism (Lopez 2000).

There are now many more sites listed on heritage inventories at the federal, state and local levels of government for their association with migration. But as with the earlier-recorded sites, they are discursively framed according to a nation-bound, 'bordered' conception of post-arrival migrant existence. Like its counterparts in Canada and the USA, this framing stresses the contribution immigrants have made to the migrant-receiving nation and minimises or discursively effaces the ongoing presence so many of them have in the sending nation and their active role in producing its built environment.[3] This depiction jars with the understanding, now well established in the field of migration studies, of migrants as transnational, diasporic subjects who, in Cohen's (2011: 5) words, 'recognize themselves as participants in multiple national communities, albeit not equally or in the same way, as well as in a community that transcends the nation.' The reification of the national border as a container of migrant heritage perhaps explains why points of arrival or touch-down are often celebrated as heritage sites, Australian examples being the Quarantine Station and Woolloomooloo Finger Wharf, both in Sydney, as well as the sites of the many migrant hostels across the country that in the 1950s and 1960s housed post-war immigrants until they found jobs and homes of their own.[4] The narrative emphasis on settlement displaces cross-border mobility to the past: these people are construed as *once* mobile, now *settled* citizens (Caglar 2016: 957).

I turn in the next section to the approach taken in China to the heritage of overseas migration, before coming back in subsequent sections to discuss alternatives to the bordered orientation to migrant heritage outlined earlier. These alternatives proceed on the basis of what might be called a mobilities ontology.

Heritage and Chineseness: China's diaspora strategy

Zhongshan was the origin place of a significant proportion of Chinese who migrated to Australia between the 1850s and 1940s (see Chapter 2). Though measuring only some 40 kilometres north to south and 30 kilometres east to west, it contains nearly 80 villages, many of which sent large numbers of their residents – overwhelmingly men – to Australia beginning in the mid-19th century. The built environment of these villages is notable for the houses constructed there by overseas Chinese for their relatives (principally wives and children) to live in and as dwellings they themselves could inhabit temporarily on return visits or permanently when they retired. The architectural style of the houses evolved over the decades from modest reworkings of the local vernacular to dramatically new designs based on the European neoclassical (Chapter 3). The effect of emigration on the materiality of the villages can also be seen in the ancestral halls and temples that were built or renovated with diaspora funding (Chapter 4) and in the modern schools that many villages acquired by the same means (Cheng 2020). These buildings, along with the grander of the remittance houses, remain stand-out features in the old core areas of the villages. Larger structures built in the post-Mao era (from the late 1970s onward), including factories and apartment buildings, tend to be located in an expanded periphery around the inner core. The core-periphery distinction shows up clearly in satellite imagery (e.g., Google Earth) particularly because the iron roofs of factory buildings in this part of southern China are almost invariably light blue in colour.

Over the last two decades, prefectural and district-level governments, along with village leaders, have come to regard as heritage assets the migrant-associated buildings belonging to the century or so prior to the founding of the People's Republic of China (PRC) in 1949. They have listed the buildings on heritage inventories and they regulate their protection. The scale of this heritage is indicated by a recent survey conducted by officials of one of Zhongshan's districts, which identified 570 pre-1949 'overseas' (diaspora-built) houses across just 4 of the 30 or so emigrant villages of

Zhongshan.[5] Most of them were grand houses built in neoclassical or (to a much lesser extent) Art Deco style during the 1920s and 1930s. Although many such houses have lain vacant for decades, heritage regulations prevent them being demolished or substantially altered, and the government provides subsidies for owners to maintain them or at least prevent their further decay. In some cases, however, the owners of locked and vacant houses have been residing for many years overseas, their whereabouts and even their names unknown to officials. Owners who have remained in Zhongshan – mostly descendants of the original migrant builders – usually prefer to live in modern apartments in Shekki, Zhongshan's urban centre, or in Guangzhou, Macau or Hong Kong. The interiors of the abandoned houses vary in their degree of decay.[6] In some, thick layers of dust have accumulated and termite damage to floorboards and stairways make them hazardous to move around in. Others are remarkably intact. Often, kitchen utensils and wooden furniture remain in place, old calendars and old photographs of family members remain stuck to walls, the stalks of incense sticks burned long ago lie on the shelves of the household shrines, suitcases and old steamer trunks gather dust on top of cabinets.

Although active government involvement in preserving the material heritage of overseas migration began only a few decades ago, it has links to 'diaspora strategies' (Ho 2020) that initially focused on promoting investment by diaspora members in the economy of their home counties and villages, as part of a call to participate in the reconstruction of the homeland following the war against the Japanese (1937–1945) and the civil war between the communists and nationalists (1927–1949). With the reform era, after the death of Mao in 1976, it was extended to seeking diaspora involvement in the spheres of science and technology, education, culture and tourism. The main institution for diaspora outreach in Zhongshan, the local office of the government's Bureau of Overseas Chinese Affairs, organises tours of emigrant villages for descendants of migrants visiting Zhongshan from America, Canada, Hawaii, Australia and elsewhere who are engaged in a form of 'roots tourism' (Maruyama and Stronza 2010). It assists some of them to locate their migrant ancestor's native village, house or grave site.[7] It also publishes a magazine for circulation amongst the diaspora featuring stories on migration-related heritage sites in Zhongshan.

In working to reconnect overseas migrant descendants to their ancestral places in China, the government promotes the idea that their roots are in the 'soil' of their ancestors' native place. This is not purely an invention of the post-1949 communist state. It has an antecedent in the valorisation of native place loyalty in traditional Chinese culture, as exemplified in the native place associations that existed in Chinese cities in dynastic and republican times, providing migrants from elsewhere in the country with a home away from home and assisted them to keep in touch with their origin counties and provinces (Goodman 1995). Native place discourse was brought into modern Chinese culture partly through its role as a genre in the field of folklore studies during the Republic (Duara 2000). China's current diaspora is embodied in the idea of a genetic-cultural essence that is inalienable. Its grounding in the idea of an essential Chineseness is captured in the term 'overseas Chinese' with its connotation that, though residing outside the homeland, migrants and migrant descendants continue to be members of the 'Family of China' (*Qinging Zhonghua*) (Liu and van Dongen 2016: 813).

China's diaspora strategy has been criticised for invoking the idea of a Greater China (Callahan 2005) and for bringing coercive pressure on diasporic Chinese to retain loyalty to China and the PRC, the two elided. But as Liu and van Dongen (2016: 820) argue, the diaspora is by no means a passive recipient of the strategy. The diversity of positions that Chinese migrants and their descendants take up in formulating their individual identities is stressed by Ien Ang (2001; 2013) who characterises Chineseness as a 'murky' and 'ambiguous' space in which a multitude of subjectivities flourish. This agrees well with what Zhongshanese migrants and descendants recently interviewed in Sydney had to say on the question of identity.[8] Most of them situated their identity in the fluid space between China and Australia. Their various degrees of interest in and attachment to heritage sites in Zhongshan tended to be framed more in terms of family and lineage-group history than anything resembling official or professional heritage discourse emanating from either China or Australia.

The Bureau of Overseas Chinese Affairs in Zhongshan presents a view of homeland heritage places as a vital constituent of the diaspora's identity and belonging. It conceives the material heritage of Chinese overseas – gold mining camps, market gardens, old shops and temples, for example – as being continuous with the heritage of the migrants' ancestral villages, including the remittance-built houses, graveyards and ancestral halls present there. This pulls in the opposite direction, as it were, to the nation-centric framing of migrant heritage in destination countries such as Australia. That framing, as described earlier, posits Chinese migrant heritage in unilinear terms as representing the progressive integration of migrants into the geo-social corpus of their new home, the adoptive nation, which is seen to be the exclusive site of their belonging. Yet the differences between the two are less than they may seem at first glance: both are nationalist in orientation. The Chinese model, far from being internationalist, invokes an extended version of the nation. The 'heritage corridor' approach to migration heritage advocated in this book presents the alternative of a heritage approach that escapes the nation-state 'container' frame.

Streets at either end of the heritage corridor

Two streets, situated at either end of the Zhongshan–Australia migration corridor, loom large in the history of Zhongshanese migration. They are Dixon Street in the heart of Sydney's Chinatown and Sunwen Zhong Lu (Figure 6.1) in the old heart of Zhongshan city (formerly the county town, Shekki). There is a sense in which these two streets are continuous with one another: many of the same people have walked along them, dined, shopped and done business in them. Some of the remittance firms based in Dixon Street also had branches in Shekki. And finally, museums dedicated to Chinese migration will soon exist on both of the streets.

As heritage sites, neither street makes complete sense without the other. For Lefebvre (1991: 261), the repetitive, rhythmic gestures of bodies, including those gestures comprising the act of walking, do not simply take place in particular spaces, they are generative of them. Whatever the physical, architectural differences between them – and they are considerable – the streets are an embodiment of the lives lived along them, lives that, for all the geographic distance separating them, were marked by a considerable degree of simultaneity. What is called for a practice of heritage that is adequate to representing such transnational simultaneity.

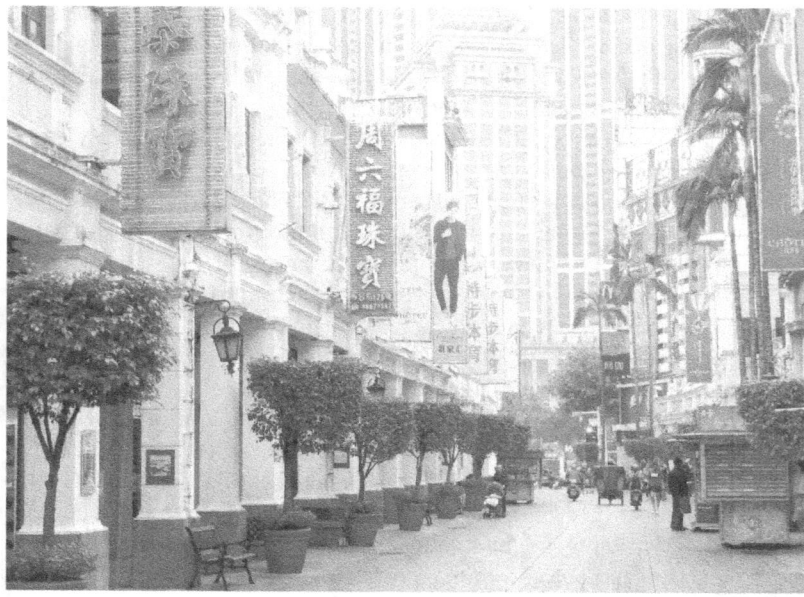

Figure 6.1 Sunwen Zhong Lu, looking east, arcaded shophouses on the left.

A salient commonality between the streets lies in their involvement in remittance transactions. By 1930, the Kwong War Chong company in Dixon Street had a branch of its remittance business in Shekki, very likely situated on Sunwen Zhong Lu. Mei-fen Kuo (2018: 162–163) lists six Chinese remittance firms in Sydney which between 1850 and 1916 had branches or partner businesses in Shekki. Remittances bound for Zhongshan County, most of them up until the time of World War I in the form of gold sovereigns and gold dust (Kuo 2018: 170), were carried to Hong Kong by ship and then up through the delta to Shekki by smaller boats which docked at the end of Sunwen Zhong Lu where it meets the Xi River. Remittances were by far the major source of Zhongshan's prosperity in the late decades of the 1800s and the early decades of the 1900s, a prosperity marked along Sunwen Zhong Lu by modern three- or four-storey commercial buildings with street-level arcades allowing pedestrians to move along the street sheltered from the sun and rain. As with similar modern thoroughfares in emigrant towns such as Xiamen, Shantou and Guangzhou that were also enriched with funds remitted from overseas, this was an architecture inspired by that of Southeast Asia's port cities, such as Singapore (Cook 2014: 140). Among the buildings erected on Sunwen Zhong Lu during this period were those built by the Sincere and the Wing On companies founded in Sydney by Zhongshan immigrants. They include a hotel, a bank and a department store (Figure 6.2). One of these grand structures now houses the Zhongshan Museum of Commercial Culture (Chapter 5). Another museum, situated further east on Sunwen Zhong Lu and focusing on Zhongshan's history of overseas migration, opened in 2021. A museum of Chinese migration, proposed as part of a building development in Dixon street, is discussed in the following section.

The buildings along the half-kilometre of Sunwen Zhong Lu closest to the river were subject to a major restoration project in the 1990s, sponsored by the Zhongshan government and reflecting a new-found appreciation of its heritage value as one of Zhongshan's main examples of 'overseas Chinese' architecture and its potential as a drawcard for tourists, including those from the diaspora.[9] Along with the policy of protecting surviving remittance houses of the pre-1949 era, the street's restoration accords with the government's 'diaspora strategies' discussed earlier, which celebrate ties to the Zhongshan 'family' overseas. In Dixon Street in Sydney's Chinatown, by comparison, no efforts at architectural conservation or restoration had been made until the current proposal to preserve the Kwong War Chong & Co building, discussed later. I attribute this to the old buildings of Dixon Street, though they have been long occupied by Chinese–Australians, being in a style of Anglo-Australian commercial architecture (dating to the late 1800s and early- to mid-1900s) which is at odds with what in Western eyes is

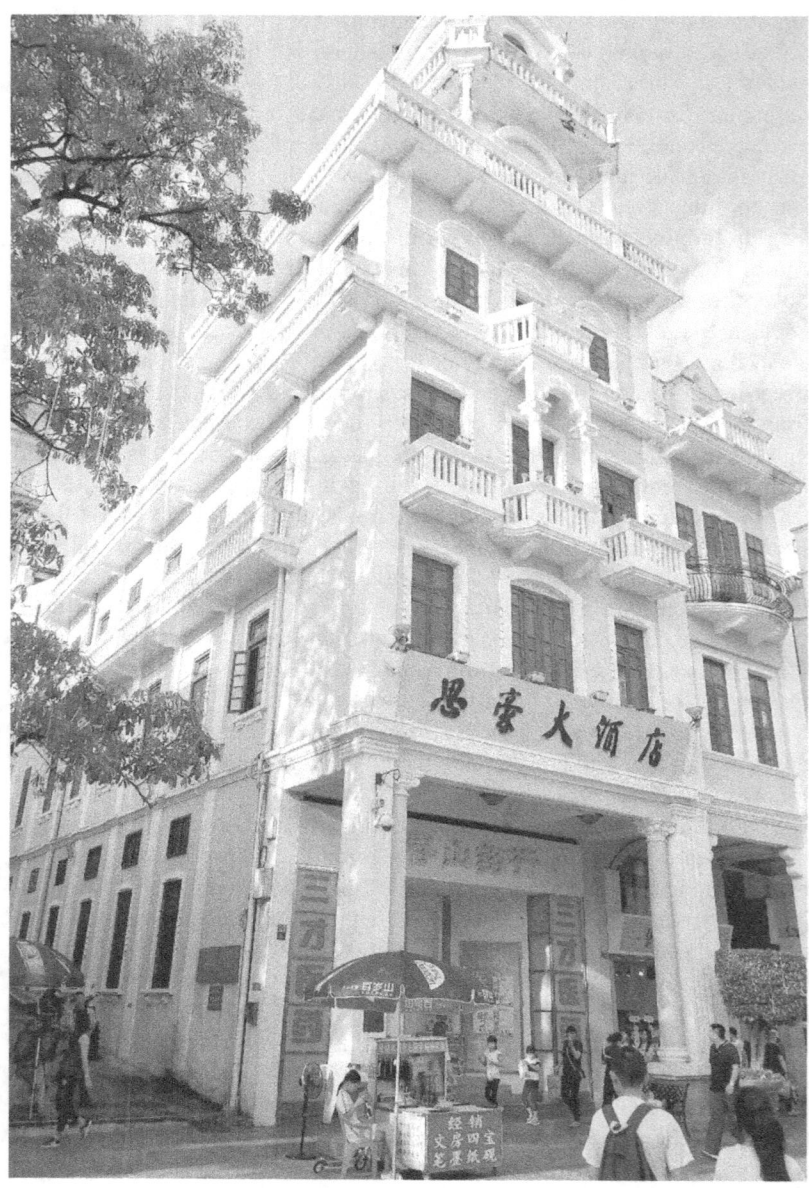

Figure 6.2 A hotel built by the Wing On company in Sunwen Zhong Lu in the early decades of the 20th century. The exterior was heavily restored in the 1990s.

authentically Chinese. Their failure to evoke the Oriental-exotic has been compensated for by the installation of an Orientalist decorative veneer, as discussed in the previous chapter.

The difference between these two orientations to the heritage of the streets is stark: Sunwen Zhong Lu celebrated for its association with modern-era transnational migration; Dixon Street subjected to an Orientalist makeover referencing a mythical ancient Chinese past and ignoring the street's history of transnational connectivity. The heritage makeover of Sunwen Zhong Lu may seem more in line with the transnational connections between the two streets and the proposition that, situated at either end of the China–Australia migration corridor, they in a sense run into each other. But the plaques attached to many of the columns of the arcades fronting both sides of the street, which provide information on the its history, make no reference to the lives of Zhongshanese overseas or how, through their business activities and their remittance-sending, these lives are embodied in the street's historical fabric.

A museum of migrant mobility

The Orientalist makeover of Dixon Street in the 1970s (Figure 6.3) was ostensibly about celebrating the heritage of Sydney's sizeable population of ethnic Chinese, which stood at almost half a million people in 2016, but in fact it had nothing to do with the actual lives of the early wave of Chinese migrants who arrived between the early 1900s and the 1940s, or of the second wave who began arriving in the 1980s. Rather, it was about the representation of a Chineseness that always had far more to do with the Western imaginary than the lived reality of Chinese persons in Australia (Chapter 5). In 2019, a proposal to demolish a three-storey commercial building in Dixon Street, dating from 1910, was opposed by a loosely affiliated group of Chinese and non-Chinese citizens on the grounds of its significance to the early-to-mid 20th-century history of Chinese migration. What was particularly significant to them was the building's association with Kwong War Chong & Co, which as well as importing and retailing Chinese goods had acted as an agency for remitting money back to China from people who had migrated from Zhongshan County (Williams 2005). The firm also arranged steamship tickets for visits home by these migrants, organised the paperwork for their dealings with the Australian immigration authorities, and, in the case of many of those who died in Australia, arranged for their remains to be repatriated to their home villages in Zhongshan (Williams 2005). Lum Chun Lee, owner of the building at 84 Dixon Street and senior partner in the firm, which he founded in 1883 and which continued to operate from the same building until 1987, was himself from Zhongshan, having arrived from there in 1874.

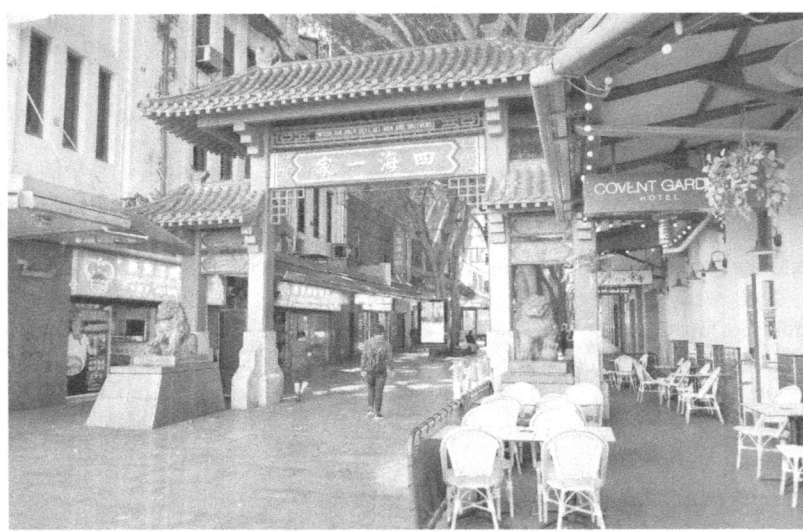

Figure 6.3 Dixon Street in Sydney's Chinatown, showing the ceremonial gateway erected in the 1970s.

A detailed report on the architecture and interior fittings of the building in Dixon Street was prepared in 2019 and the building was entered on the New South Wales Heritage Inventory (Figure 6.4).[10] In 2020, the new owners of the building, on the recommendation of their heritage consultants, proposed to retain and conserve it within the envelope of a development that included a neighbouring block of land. It was proposed that the two upper floors of the former Kwong War Chong & Co building be turned into a 'Chinese Australian museum.'[11]

In discussing here the form such a museum might take, inspiration has been drawn from Tim Ingold's meshwork concept (Ingold 2007, 2013, 2017). Building on the work of Deleuze and Guattari (2004), Ingold proposes that we think of social life as lived along 'lines of becoming' which, like trails, are formed by the histories and trajectories of individual lives. These lines interweave and entangle with other such lifelines to form what Ingold calls a meshwork. The points in the meshwork at which lines converge are referred to by Ingold as 'knots', and I suggest we think of buildings as being one of the forms that knots can take. Ingold sees the lines and the points at which they meet as representing stories that intertwine.

> The storied world is a world of movement and becoming, in which anything, caught at a particular place and moment, enfolds within its

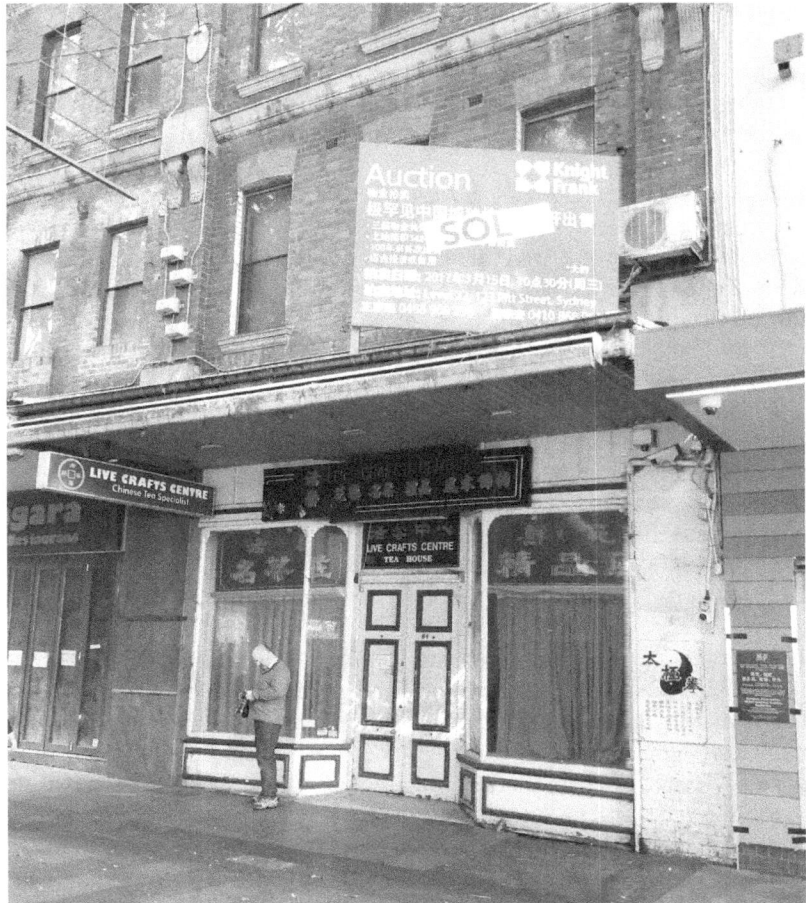

Figure 6.4 The former Kwong War Chong & Co building in Dixon Street, Sydney.

constitution the history of relations that have brought it there. We can only tell the nature of things by attending to their relations, by telling their stories. For the things of the world are their stories, identified by their paths of movement in an unfolding field of relations. Things occur where things meet, occurrences intertwine, as each becomes bound up in the other's story.

(Ingold 2011: 159–161)

It is suggested here that the proposed museum at 84 Dixon Street become a museum of Chinese migrant movement and becoming that tells stories from the meshwork of trajectories that the building was woven into. A number of points of understanding would inform such an undertaking, one of which is that the building itself, in all its material solidity, should not be allowed to dominate but rather should always be seen as just one point in a meshwork of transnational proportions.

We know that many Zhongshanese men working as market gardeners in suburban Sydney and regional New South Wales brought a portion of their earnings to the Kwong War Chong & Co office to have them sent back as remittances to their relatives in Zhongshan. Some of those visiting China-town from market gardens in distant locations stayed overnight in a 'dormitory' on an upper floor of the 84 Dixon Street building. The dormitory also served as a staging point on their periodic visits back to their home villages in China, via Hong Kong. Rather than thinking of the building as a central point with lines radiating out from it – for example, to market gardens – it should be understood as a 'knot', in Ingold's terminology, one among the multitude of knots making up the meshwork, included among them the market gardens themselves. Whether the lines of the mesh represent the movement of people, money or of the goods traded by Kwong War Chong & Co, they do not end at the Dixon Street building, they simply pause there before moving on: 'every line overtakes the knot in which it is tied' (Ingold 2013: 132). Multiple lines entangle in and at the building, in the way that individual lines of rope or string embrace and circle each other to form a knot before disentangling and moving on. While the individual lines (and the life trajectories that formed them) retain their integrity in the meshwork, they are also defined by their relations with other lifelines.

For the proposed museum to succeed in giving visibility to the meshwork constituted by Chinese migrancy, it must overcome the long-embedded tendency in heritage practice to give undue weight to buildings, as compared to more subtle material traces, in representing past lives. At times it seems as if the more physical heft a built structure has the more weight it carries in the heritage stakes: the cathedral, for example, eclipses the wayside shrine. In a closely related way, heritage practice also gives priority to stasis over mobility, to settled over mobile lifeways. It is easy to see how, by way of these habits of heritage practice, migrant lives will have less visibility in heritage inventories than the more 'settled' lives of the non-migrant population. Translating all this into the terms of Ingold's meshwork, the knots of the mesh are given prominence over the lines. The professional practice of heritage and the state governance around it – consisting, for example, of heritage protection legislation and heritage listing mechanisms – seem inherently biased towards knots (in the form of buildings and spatially circumscribed sites) at the expense of the lines running between them.

Another understanding that is key to achieving a museum that does justice to migrant mobility is that the lines of the meshwork are constituted by the movement of objects as well as by people. The Chinese market gardener brings his cabbages, lettuce, tomatoes and cucumbers to the markets in Chinatown where they are exchanged for cash, some of which he then takes to the nearby Kwong War Chong & Co office at 84 Dixon Street to be remitted back to Zhongshan. The remittances might be sent in the form of gold, but bank drafts were more commonly used by the 1930s for those sent from Australia (Williams 2018: 101). Remittances were generally accompanied by *qiaopi* (letters) from the sender (Benton, Liu and Zhang 2021). While the sender returned to his market garden, the remittance funds and *qiaopi* moved on to Zhongshan (via Hong Kong) inscribing their own trajectory or 'line' in the meshwork, separate from yet continuous with that of the market gardener. These 'object lines', which helped extend the meshwork transnationally, passed through a series of knots which, in the earlier case, included the Kwong War Chong & Co's offices (or its agents' offices) in Hong Kong and Zhongshan, until they came to rest in the hands of the recipient in the migrant's home village. There, as shown in Chapter 3, the remittances often congealed in the form of the new houses they paid for. The remittances might be said to project the market gardener's agency out through the Zhongshan–Australia migration corridor, meaning the new house in the village was partly a projection of him. Such projections helped form and animate a meshwork of transnational proportions. Imagine for a moment how the new house in the village may have had its origin in the dreams of the market gardener: waking dreams he entertains as he waters his rows of vegetables or dreams which occupy his sleep as he lies in his hut at night. They are dreams that project certain futures out through the meshwork.

The museum I am foreshadowing would treat the meshwork as open–ended; it would not try to totalise the stories of the migrants whose lifelines momentarily converged and passed on through the building which houses it. The museum, as it is imagined here, is a dispersed entity – it melts into the meshwork it gives visibility to. It does not *collect* things in the way museums typically do – it *follows* them. Using the rich array of electronic media museums now have at their disposal, the museum would permit the visitor to escape the spatial and temporal limits that heritage work too often imposes. It would set out to honour the kind of cross-border fluidity that this book has attempted to represent.

A meshwork approach has been offered here as a means to foster a heritage representation that is true to the fluidity of migrancy, but there are other ways this can happen. For example, the professional field of heritage practice could begin to attend to the heritage-making projects that thousands of migrant descendants worldwide have embarked upon. These people undertake journeys and cross borders as they retrace the trajectories of migrant parents, grandparents or more remote ancestors. They locate and visit ancestral homes, villages and graveyards and expose themselves to the medley of affects and emotions that accompany the experience of being in these places. For our part, we can do more to interrogate and refuse the methodological nationalism which so limits our ability to engage with the material past of migrant lives.

Notes

1 Long-term permanent departure of residents from Australia (defined as departing for more than one year) rose from 21,296 in 1959 to 52,027 in 1969. www. aph.gov.au/binaries/library/pubs/bn/sp/migrationpopulation.pdf.
2 For example, Alister Bowen (2012: 7–8) provides a summary of archaeological research on sites relating to Chinese presence in Australia.
3 See, for example, in Canada, the Museum of Migration www.pier21.ca/home; in the USA, the Angel Island Immigration Station Foundation www.aiisf.org/. See also McShane's (2001: 129) comment on 'the suitcase as a design gesture in migration exhibitions.'
4 For the Quarantine Station, see www.quarantinestation.com.au/About-Us/; for migrant hostels in New South Wales, see www.migrationheritage.nsw.gov.au/ exhibition/aplaceforeveryone/migrant-hostels-in-nsw/. See McShane's (2001: 130–131) critical comments on the notion of the Quarantine Station as a migration museum.
5 Information conveyed during a meeting with district officials in December 2017.
6 These observations were made during fieldwork in Zhongshan's emigrant villages between 2017 and 2019.
7 In the 19th and early-20th centuries, the remains of Chinese migrants who died overseas were often returned to their natal village for burial in the clan cemetery, those repatriated to Zhongshan going by way of Hong Kong (Fitzgerald 2007: Sinn 2013: 265–297).
8 Interviews conducted in 2017–2019 by Ien Ang, Denis Byrne, Alexandra Wong and Christopher Cheng, see www.heritagecorridor.org.au.
9 The restoration of the buildings, which involved resurfacing the entirety of their façades with a thick layer of cement render, would be considered 'heavy handed' according to heritage best-practice conventions originating in the West but is in keeping with the traditional practice of restoring temples in China (Byrne 2014: 95–103).
10 'Former Kwong War Chong & Company building, including interiors and contents of No. 84,' unpublished document, NSW Office of Environment and Heritage. https://apps.environment.nsw.gov.au/dpcheritageapp/ViewHeritage-ItemDetails.aspx?ID=5067050.
11 Heritage Impact Statement, Nos. 82–84 Dixon Street & 413–415 Sussex Street, Haymarket. Prepared by Weir Phillips Heritage and Planning, December 2020. Unpublished report.

References

Anderson, Benedict. 1991. *Imagined Communities: Reflections on the Origin and Spread of Nationalism*. Ithaca, NY: Cornell University Press.

Ang, Ien. 2001. *On Not Speaking Chinese: Living Between Asia and the West*. London: Routledge.

Ang, Ien. 2013. 'No longer Chinese? Residual Chineseness after the rise of China,' in Julia Kuehn, Kam Louie, and David M. Pomfret (eds.), *Diasporic Chineseness After the Rise of China: Communities and Cultural Production*, pp. 17–31. Vancouver: University of British Columbia.

Benton, Gregor, Hong Liu and Huimei Zhang. 2021. *The Qiaopi Trade and Transnational Networks in the Chinese Diaspora*. London: Routledge.

Bowen, Alister M. 2012. *Archaeology of the Chinese Fishing Industry in Colonial Victoria*. Sydney: Sydney University Press.

Byrne, Denis. 2014. *Counterheritage: Critical Perspectives on Heritage Conservation in Asia*. New York: Routledge.

Byrne, Denis. 2016. 'The need for a transnational approach to the material heritage of migration: The China-Australia heritage corridor,' *Journal of Social Archaeology* 16(3): 261–285, https://doi.org/10.1177/1469605316673005.

Caglar, Ayse. 2016. 'Still "migrants" after all those years: Foundational mobilities, temporal frames and emplacement of migrants,' *Journal of Ethnic and Migration Studies* 42(6): 952–969, https://doi.org/10.1080/1369183X.2015.1126085.

Callahan, William A. 2005. 'Nationalism, civilization and transnational relations: The discourse of Greater China,' *Journal of Contemporary China* 14(43): 269–289, https://doi.org/10.1080/10670560500065629.

Cheng, Christopher. 2020. 'Beacons of modern learning: Diaspora-funded schools in the China-Australia corridor,' *Asian and Pacific Migration Journal* 29(2): 139–162, https://doi.org/10.1177/0117196820930309.

Cohen, Deborah. 2011. *Braceros: Migrant Citizens and Transnational Subjects in the Postwar United States and Mexico*. Chapel Hill, NC: University of North Carolina Press.

Cook, James, A. 2014. 'Rethinking "China": Overseas Chinese and China's modernity,' in James A. Cook, Joshua Goldstein, Mathew D. Johnson, and Sigrid Schmalzer (eds.), *Visualizing Modern China*, pp. 127–143. Lanham, MD: Lexington Books.

Deleuze, Gilles and Felix Guattari. 2004. *A Thousand Plateaus: Capitalism and Schizophrenia*. Translated from the French by Brian Massumi. London: Continuum.

Duara, Prasenjit. 2000. 'Local worlds: The poetics and politics of native place in China,' *The South Atlantic Quarterly* 99(1): 13–45, https://doi.org/10.1215/003 82876-99-1-13.

Fitzgerald, John. 2007. *Big White Lie: Chinese Australians in White Australia*. Sydney: University of New South Wales Press.

Foster, Lois and David Stockley. 1984. *Multiculturalism: The Changing Australian Paradigm*. Clevedon: Multilingual Matters.

Goodman, Bryna. 1995. *Native Place, City, and Nation: Regional Networks and Identities in Shanghai, 1853–1937*. Berkeley: University of California Press.

Hamilakis, Yannis. 2007. *The Nation and Its Ruins: Antiquity, Archaeology and National Imagination in Greece*. Oxford: Oxford University Press.

Handler, Richard. 1988. *Nationalism and the Politics of Culture in Quebec*. Madison, WI: University of Wisconsin Press.

Ho, Elaine. 2020 'Leveraging connectivities: Comparative diaspora strategies and evolving cultural pluralities in China and Singapore,' *American Behavioural Scientist* 64(10): 1415–1429, https://doi.org/10.1177/0002764220947754.

Ingold, Tim. 2007. *Lines: A Brief History*. London: Routledge.

Ingold, Tim. 2011. *Being Alive. Essays on Movement, Knowledge and Description*. New York: Routledge.

Ingold, Tim. 2013. *Making: Anthropology, Archaeology, Art and Architecture*. London: Routledge.

Ingold, Tim. 2017. 'On human correspondence,' *Journal of the Royal Anthropological Institute* 23(1): 9–27, https://doi.org/10.1111/1467-9655.12541.

Kuo, Mei-fen. 2018. 'Jinxin: The remittance trade and enterprising Chinese Australians, 1850–1916,' in Gregor Benton, Hong Liu and Huimei Zhang (eds.), *The Qiaopi Trade and Transnational Networks in the Chinese Diaspora*, pp. 169–175. London: Routledge.

Lefebvre, Henri. 1991. *The Production of Space*. Translated from the French by Donald Nicholson-Smith. Oxford: Blackwell.

Levitt, Peggy and Nina Glick Schiller. 2004. 'Conceptualizing simultaneity: A transnational social field perspective on society,' *International Migration Review* 38(3): 1002–1039, https://doi.org/10.1111/j.1747-7379.2004.tb00227.x.

Liu, Hong and Els van Dongen. 2016. 'China's diaspora policies as a new mode of transnational governance,' *Journal of Contemporary China* 25(102): 805–821, https://doi.org/10.1080/10670564.2016.1184894.

Lopez, Mark. 2000. *The Origins of Multiculturalism in Australian Politics, 1945–1975*. Melbourne: Melbourne University Press.

Maruyama, Naho and Amanda Stronza. 2010. 'Roots tourism of Chinese Americans,' *Ethnology* 49(1): 23–44.

McShane, Ian. 2001. 'Challenging or conventional? Migration history in Australian Museums,' in Darryl McIntyre, and Kirsten Wehner (eds.), *National Museums, Negotiated Histories*, pp. 122–132. Canberra: National Museum of Australia.

Purdie, R. W. 1997. *The Register of the National Estate: Who, What, Where?* Canberra: Australian Heritage Commission.

Sheller, Mimi. 2003. 'Creolization in discourses of global culture,' in Sara Ahmed, Claudia Castada, Anne-Marie Fortier and Mimi Sheller (eds.), *Uprootings/Regroundings: Questions of Home and Migration*, pp. 273–294. Oxford: Berg.

Sinn, Elizabeth. 2013. *Pacific Crossing: California Gold, Chinese Migration, and the Making of Hong Kong*. Hong Kong: Hong University Press.

Williams, Michael. 2005. 'Historical notes on 82–85 Dixon Street,' unpublished document.

Williams, Michael. 2018. *Returning Home with Glory: Chinese Villagers Around the Pacific, 1849 to 1949*. Hong Kong: Hong Kong University Press.

Winichakul, Thongchai. 1994. *Siam Mapped: A History of the Geobody of Siam*. Honolulu: University of Hawai'i Press.

Winter, Tim. 2015. 'Heritage and Nationalism: An unbreachable couple?' in Emma Waterton and Steve Watson (eds.), *The Palgrave Handbook of Contemporary Heritage Research*, pp. 331–345. London: Palgrave Macmillan, https://doi.org/10.1057/9781137293565_21.

Index

Note: Page numbers in *italics* indicate a figure on the corresponding page.

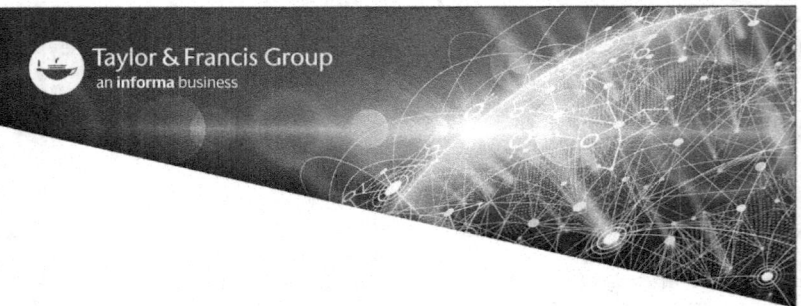
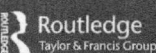 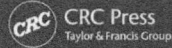

For Product Safety Concerns and Information please contact our EU
representative GPSR@taylorandfrancis.com
Taylor & Francis Verlag GmbH, Kaufingerstraße 24, 80331 München, Germany